SILVER THREADS

SILVER THREADS

Critical Reflections on Growing Old

Doris Marshall

between the lines

© Between The Lines 1987

Published by Between The Lines
229 College Street
Toronto, Ontario M5T 1R4

Cover design by Art Work
Cover photographs by Deborah Barndt
Typeset by Coach House Press, Toronto
Printed in Canada

Between The Lines
receives financial assistance from the Canada Council, the
Ontario Arts Council, and the Department of Communications.

Canadian Cataloguing in Publication Data

Marshall, Doris, 1911-
    Silver threads

ISBN 0-919946-80-1 (bound).
ISBN 0-919946-81-X (pbk.)

1. Marshall, Doris, 1911-.
2. Aging – Social aspects – Canada.
3. Aged – Canada.
4. Social work with the aged – Canada.
I. Title.

HQ1064.C3M37 1987   305.2'6'0971   C87-093620-4

for Brenda and Oliver, Naomi and Karl,
Judith, Mary and Jama

and for my other family, past and present, immediate and
gathered, from different parts of the world ...
from whom and with whom I've learned so much

especially I remember the late Rae Abenethy,
whose knowledge and energy in the field of aging
sparked my own continuing interest and efforts

Contents

Acknowledgements

TO ACKNOWLEDGE suitably the help I have received along the way of writing a first book seems a monumental undertaking. Over more than three-quarters of a century, gleanings – from the historical, experiential, and analytical points of view – have given me so much. My sincere thanks for all that has contributed in any way to the depth and meaning of my reflections on aging.

Specifically, I am glad for the family into which – with my sister and six brothers – I was born, and with whom my earliest years were spent. Along with the struggle for survival the importance of education, books, music, and good neighbourliness was planted in my mind.

When I began to consider the possibilities of writing a book on aging, I was encouraged by the support of my friends and colleagues at the Development Education Centre, Toronto. The fact that Between The Lines, a publishing house partly owned by DEC, agreed to publish my book and that Robert Clarke would be the editor gave me a real sense of pleasurable security. Jamie Swift, formerly of DEC, had assisted me with other writing and said he would help to get me started. Several years of writing and rewriting found us with a huge heap of pages needing to be put into some kind of workable shape. Arlene Moscovitch came to our aid and in her usual capable way did the job.

From the beginning, Dr. Sheila Neysmith was most generous in responding to our need for clarification on the issues of pensions and income security. Her thoughtful criticism and continued encouragement call for hearty thanks, indeed. Rhea Shulman, director of the Bernard Betel Centre for Creative Living, helped greatly with her insightful comments on the importance of the multi-service centre as an alternative to institutional care for old people. Stimulation also came from Musza Halper, who phoned me every week to see if I was working and to urge me to hurry.

There are many others who also contributed much-needed help: among them, the librarians in the Toronto public libraries – Metro, Northern District, and Spadina; Ben Carniol of the Ryerson Polytechnical Institute's School of Social Work; Cynthia Kelly, R.N., of Rhode Island; Dr. Russ McNeil, Toronto; and Dr. Michael Watson, Edmonton. I am also grateful for financial assistance received from the Canada Council Explorations Program.

Above all I wish to voice my appreciation and thanks to Jamie Swift, who saw the project through from beginning to end. His encouragement and steadfast work are beyond measure.

Again, my thanks to all of you – individuals and groups – for your help. For the final interpretation and commentary on what you have given me, I take full responsibility.

D.M., April 1987

1

Introduction

Before the end of the second world war few studies of aging or the aged in industrial societies had been carried out by social scientists.... It was left to a doctor, J.H. Sheldon (later to become president of the International Association of Gerontology) to produce, as late as 1947, the first really perceptive account of the social problems of the elderly. Since then, in the short span of less than twenty years, the number of studies has swollen rapidly from a trickle to a modest stream and, at least in the United States, to an impressive flood.... This explosion of interest must not be applauded uncritically.

PETER TOWNSEND, at the First Canadian Conference
on Aging, 1966

IN 1981 THE CANADIAN Association on Gerontology and the Gerontological Society of America held a joint meeting in a couple of downtown Toronto hotels. It was not my first experience of such a gathering. In 1970 the province of Ontario, on behalf of other Canadian provinces, welcomed "all Fellows, Members, Students and Guests to the 23rd annual meeting of the Gerontological Society" in the Royal York Hotel in Toronto. At the close of that event, I was one of a small number of Canadians who met informally to discuss the formation of a group that would try to bring together the many people and organizations addressing the situation of aging in Canada.

And now in 1981, here I was attending the 34th Annual Scientific meeting of the Gerontological Society of America, and the 10th Annual Scientific and Educational Meeting of the Canadian Association on Gerontology / Association canadienne de gérontologie. I tried to catch as many sessions of the meetings as possible, rushing back and forth in the labyrinth of underground tunnels connecting the seminar rooms, meeting old friends and making new ones. In the midst of all the bustle I found myself sitting in a quiet and rather dimly-lit ballroom beside a young woman I knew.

We were there to listen to a session on geriatric assessment services. As one of the participants moved to the lectern to begin his presentation, my companion whispered, "He's a nice, honest fellow." I nodded in agreement, for I had known Dr. Jack MacDonell for a long time. We had both been involved with the Age and Opportunity Bureau in Winnipeg in the early 1960s, well before the first Canadian Conference on Aging in 1966.

The Bureau, set up as an education and information centre for the elderly, was founded in 1957 to meet the needs of those old people who had flooded to the city from the family farms that no longer seemed to have any place for them. In 1959 I met the A&O's director, the late Rae Abernethy and through her, "Dr. Jack", as she affectionately called Dr. MacDonell.

As I sat and thought and listened in the quiet that envelops a gathering when a person speaks with depth and sincerity, tears came to my eyes. My companion noticed and asked if I was alright. I assured her I was, but began to wonder: Why was I crying?

Afterwards I mulled over the experience, trying to understand the feelings – such intense feelings – that had swept over me at the meeting. My reaction, I finally realized, came from a deep sadness triggered by the memories that Dr. MacDonell's presence evoked.

I identified Dr. MacDonell with the beginnings of my own work in the field of aging more than twenty years before. My sadness was caused by the agonizing slowness of any movement towards a more just and humane way of dealing with life in the later years. It was and still is a sadness mixed with anger, because I fear that our "advances" in bureaucratic structures and research opportunities in the now popular field of aging may lead us even further away from the goal of enhancing the quality of life available to the elderly. Will this kind of progress simply continue to categorize old people as "problems" that make necessary the delivery of certain services? Such questions are all too familiar to me.

During my years of work as an organizer of church and community programs for the elderly, I experienced a steadily rising feeling of unease about the way society treats old people. For a long time I had trouble getting my mind around the cause of this complex problem, but the nagging doubts persisted. I knew from personal experience as a woman raised on a farm and working in the north that many other people in Canada had little control over their own lives. Farm women and Native people shared the same powerlessness experienced by old people. It was only when I became officially "Old" in society's eyes and continued to work on the problems of old people that I began to see with more clarity *why* we were in such a bad state.

I now believe that quality of life in the later years is not possible in a world where a mechanistic mentality dominates, where old systems of family and neighbourhood no longer exist, where "things" take precedence over human well-being. In my work with old and young people, it has become very clear that we must discover new family and neighbourhood relationships in which caring about and helping one another and fighting together for just and fair treatment for all would be the rallying point for a different kind of extended family.

And so, after many years of formulating these concerns in work with the aged – giving courses in retirement preparation, organizing group programs, working in a residence for the elderly, helping to develop alternative types of educational materials about aging – I have chosen to write about old age and old people as we approach the twenty-first century. I hope that in so doing it will be possible to see, through the prism of my lifetime, how the way we live our lives has changed over the years, and what must be done if old people are, in fact, to see themselves and be seen as persons of worth and value.

2

The Realities of Growing Old

At last I understood that the way over, or through this dilemma, the unease at writing about 'petty personal problems' was to recognise that nothing is personal, in the sense that it is uniquely one's own. Writing about oneself, one is writing about others, since your problems, pains, pleasures, emotions – and your extraordinary and remarkable ideas – can't be yours alone ... growing up is after all only the understanding that one's unique and incredible experience is what everyone shares.

DORIS LESSING, *The Golden Notebook*

SHE WAS DRESSED in a baggy pantsuit and one of those heavy outdoor cardigan sweaters with a football player emblazoned on the back. I saw her as she walked, painfully slowly, along a side street carrying a plastic shopping bag. The most striking thing was how stooped over she was. She might have been suffering from some sort of spinal disorder; although she was not especially short she seemed tiny, almost lost in the bulky sweater.

It was another poor old woman. She paused to open her battered white vinyl purse and carefully counted out a bunch of bills. Maybe she was coming from cashing her pension cheque. Two young boys, both no older than seven or eight, came up and stopped, staring at her. She looked up from her handbag, and nervously shoved the money back inside. With a worried frown she resumed her slow shuffle.

The boys walked along behind and the smaller one shouted out, "You old crab!" The old woman tried to ignore him, but he continued to pester her. "*You're* the crab," she said. "And besides, I'm not that old."

"Then how come your hair's so dirty and messy?"

The woman continued to walk along, muttering something about the boy not being very nice and threatening to "get the police onto him". I was watching all of this from a few steps back and a block later, after more of the same, I felt I had to do something. I went up to the boys and told them they shouldn't be so mean to old people. What did they think it would be like for them when they were old some day?

"I'm never going to get old," one of them said.

Obviously, this little boy was sadly deluded. Yet what is so disturbing about this incident is not just the unthinking heartlessness of one so young. It is also that the prejudice against old people so pervasive in our society has filtered down to shape even the perceptions of children.

Ageism is a new word that has only recently entered our vocabulary, and is used mostly in reference to the later years. Like more familiar terms such as racism and sexism it refers to a way of thinking whereby huge groups of people are arbitrarily assigned restricted roles and depicted as exhibiting somewhat peculiar characteristics. Women are best suited for housework, the young are lazy and hooked on drugs, the poor are a shiftless lot, old people are crabby and ugly. Notions like these are transmitted and reinforced in a variety of ways. We get them from our parents, from the books we read, from radio and television, in the papers, through the educational system. They make up a dangerous part of the dominant ideology of our society.

The more pervasive and entrenched an ideology, the more evidence there is of it all around us. Like women, blacks, Native people, and others who have at least succeeded in making it unfashionable – if not unacceptable – to overtly express opinions and use language based on prejudices, some old people have begun to fight against the ideas and practices that put them down and keep them down.

How had the boy who was harassing the old woman on the street come by his negative ideas about old age? Where do we get our images of the doddering old fool, the constantly complaining old woman, the lovable but more than slightly addled Gramps? Why and when did old age stop being seen as the honourable culmination of a well-lived life, as the age of wisdom and experience?

Certainly the media have not served old people well. A case in point is an issue of *Maclean's* magazine that dealt with what the editors headlined as the "Coming Old Age Crisis" and hinted darkly at the possible bankruptcy of pension plans.[1] I was interested in how this mass publication would treat the usual themes of troubled times ahead for tomorrow's elderly, but what really struck me about the magazine was the picture on the cover. It depicted four profiles of the same woman, with her face dramatically changing from image to image in an apparent attempt to depict the aging process. In the first profile, in the foreground, she was bright-eyed, young, and smiling. By the fourth profile the smile and bright eye had been replaced by a firmly closed mouth and a frown. The gleam had been removed from her now baggy cye, her face was wrinkled and furrowed, her hair grey.

The cover designer had clearly decided to associate youth with happiness and vibrancy, old age with sadness and decline. As I looked at the combination of alarming headline and distressing graphics, I wondered how the "greying baby boom generation" would react. It seemed inevitable that younger people would both be reaffirmed – about the all-importance of their youth – and confirmed in their gloomy feelings about becoming old.

Citizens: Senior and Separate

As I grow older, I realize ever more clearly that aging is a biological process. I can literally feel it in my bones. So far it has had its most profound effects on my hearing. Others fall prey to degenerative diseases, such as arthritis, diabetes, or Alzheimer's Disease, perhaps even before they reach sixty. But at the same time that our bodies and sometimes our minds change, the society we live in determines the way that we – as human beings – age. When aging is seen in a negative light, as a time when we inevitably withdraw and become separate, dependent, and all too often poor, that says a lot about our society.

In recent decades, any unusual behaviour in an old person has been attributed at once to age. Even some doctors who should have known better were prone to say, "It's just your age, you know." They would prescribe some medication and dismiss the old person as quickly as possible.

For many old people, denied a proper diagnosis, advanced age is seen as a time of inevitable illness and deterioration. In point of fact, this fixed notion of old people as sick, feeble, and totally dependent is a distortion carried forward from a time when the most visible and easy-to-reach source of data was the 8 per cent of the over-sixty-five population who lived in some kind of institution.

Now, with the much greater popularity of gerontology and the availability of more money and research personnel, the falseness of such a notion is clear to those who have access to the recent findings gleaned from the broader data base. As Barry McPherson says, in his book *Aging As A Social Process*, from a time of interest in health and aging based on a "medical model" there are now a number of journal and review articles whose authors have used a "functional model" to study health and aging: "One outcome of this research has been the debunking of the myth that the elderly are frail and sickly, and that they are incapable of performing tasks or participating in social life."[2]

Old people now form the fastest-growing population group in the country, with the number of those sixty-five and over multiplying twice as fast as the general population.[3] And one of the most important points made by the 1966 Senate Committee on Aging was that many, if not most, older people enjoy relatively good health and can get around as actively as they did in their younger years.[4] More recently a federal government report on aging found that 80 per cent of people aged sixty-five and over live without need of "health service support", or "with only periodic care".[5] As Senator David Croll said in his Foreword to the Senate committee report, "Aging is a normal process that goes hand in hand with living. It is not a disease; neither is it an inborn handicap."[6]

Increasingly now, the "old age equals sick" labelling is unacceptable, as more and more knowledge of the aging process becomes available to all of us. Society has begun to see that most old people can and do remain independent, caring for themselves in their own homes and community. But, unfortunately, media images and the negative attitudes many of us have come to accept – of passivity, uselessness, and deterioration – still dominate our images of the "declining years". Sexual drives, the need to feel competent and useful, the need for intellectual, emotional, and physical stimulation – all these are assumed to be part of the distant past. No wonder then that many people prefer not to think about aging and the elderly and accept the prevailing idea of separation, which sets the old apart from family and the rest of society. How slowly we change.

Just how slowly is clear when we consider that almost twenty years after the Senate report, one of the humanitarian issues raised at the 1982 Assembly on Aging discussions in Vienna was "The confusion, by health delivery systems, of normal aging with disease leading to poor diagnosis and care plans for older persons".[7]

Over and over again I hear old people say, "We aren't sick. We don't need medical help. What we do need is affordable housing, enough money to survive, usable transportation, help with some chores and household repairs. And we still want to have something to do in our community and be in touch with other people on a daily basis."

In our culture, distances – physical, social, and spiritual – seem to separate us so that it is hard to keep our relationships alive and well. At the same time, being old seems unacceptable. Many an old person attempts to get around this problem by imitating the young: coloured hair for women, hairpieces for men; cosmetic transformations; extremely plastic measures to appear young. It seems it is a terrible thing to appear to be old. Still, "Oldness" is changing. There are so many of us. Some of us have more education, more money, better health. With our rapidly growing "population group" as a new market, the media and advertising people are beginning to highlight all the pleasures and possibilities available for the retirement years.

From the national level, through provincial and even regional areas, there are advisory bodies to assist governments in planning and carrying out projects for the elderly. Universities offer varied courses for retired people and these are usually over-crowded. Many older people use the Elderhostel programs to continue their education and see the world, to the extent that a recent Elderhostel catalogue contained 125 newsprint pages of available provincial, national, and international programs. It is not surprising that in a high school class about growing old, one of the students exclaimed to me, "Old people sure have a good time: lots of money to enjoy life"!

Canada does have an enormous number of organizations of and for old people. They exist at all levels. Some are responsible to government and others advise government. Some are non-governmental, sponsored by churches or community organizations, or set up by people on their own. Such organizations have spawned innumerable programs for old people. We can go bowling and play shuffleboard. We can learn crafts, take tours, play cards, or sing in special choirs. There are lots of university courses and continuing education programs for us to try. We can take part in theatre groups and orchestras, go to special hostels and camps.

With all this attention, surely old people must be in clover. But even a casual assessment of the situation in which we old people find ourselves tells a different story. Neither "oldness" as unacceptable nor "oldness" as pleasant opportunity really addresses the matter of aging. Each is merely the creation of an image in a changing society that puts the emphasis on individualism, consumerism, and rapid, competitive growth.

Poverty and Pensions

In Canada, to be old is to be poor. Or at least that is the case for half of us. "An astonishing number of this country's aged are poor," reported the National Council of Welfare, a government-established citizens' advisory body.

The Council found that, "by conservative estimate", in 1981 one aged Canadian in four was living on a "low income" or below the poverty line.[8] Although incomes for the aged improved slightly during the 1980s, as of January 1987 49.2 per cent of the people getting Old Age Security were also receiving a Guaranteed Income Supplement – which goes to pensioners with either no income or only a limited amount of income apart from the OAS.[9] Unattached elderly women – most of them widows – face the highest risk of poverty. Some 60 per cent of them live on a low income. (The figure for unattached elderly men is 48.1 per cent.)[10] And the statistics show that as you grow older, into your seventies and eighties, your risk of being poor, or getting poorer, continues to increase ... and increase.[11]

Our children, as they reach middle age, are likely encountering problems keeping up with mortgage payments, providing their own children with support, and generally making ends meet. In contrast to the situation when I was growing up, today both parents often have to work outside the home. They may feel they have to help us. They may try to do so in earnest. They may just feel the odd twinge of guilt and try to ignore us. Whatever the case, we are faced with the problem of caring and providing for ourselves at a time when family and kinship bonds are changing.

There is a definite emphasis on individual responsibility in Canadian society's approach to aging. If we are left to fend for ourselves, perhaps with a little help from our children, it's up to each of us to do so as individuals. The government has developed a pension system that fails to provide enough money for half of us to get over the poverty line. Many of us are *just* over that line. The latest figures available, for 1981, show that men receive an average of $2,000 and women about $900 a year from private pensions.[12] The tragedy is that still less than half of the working population is covered by private, employer-sponsored pension plans.

Whether or not we get over the poverty line depends entirely on how "well" we did earlier in our lives. While everyone is guaranteed a basic minimum income under the Old Age Security and Guaranteed Income Supplement programs, the emphasis is on *minimum*. It is far below what any citizen needs for a decent life. Earnings under the Canada Pension Plan (CPP), launched in 1966, are tied to our performance in the labour market. Women who worked in the home and did not participate in the paid labour force receive nothing from the Canada Pension Plan. My own paid work was mostly between 1959 and 1970, so I receive about $300 a month from the CPP.

The CPP, notwithstanding the fact that it covers all employees, operates basically the same as the private pension plans some Canadians contribute to during their working lives. The more you made and the more you contributed, the higher your benefits. Your material well-being when you get old depends entirely on your track record in the earlier part of your life. People who were poor in their earlier years will inevitably be even more poor when they get old. People who just managed to get by in their earlier years will more than likely slip into poverty in their seventies.

According to the pervasive individualist ethic, it is up to each of us to *perform* well enough to save money and accumulate pension plan contributions so that we can afford decent food and shelter when we get old. If we do well in the race for cash income, we are worth more when we retire. If we fail to save for the future, our destitution in old age is seen as nobody's fault but our own. We are worth much less.

Of those who *do* put money into a private plan, until very recently two workers out of three could not have their old age benefits transferred to their husbands or wives when they died

– while the private insurance business, dominated by insurance firms, trust companies, and banks, is highly profitable.

The private pension system always was, is, and will continue to be designed primarily to provide a pool of capital for financial institutions to invest. The needs of pensioners come second. This is *the* reason why the great pension debate of the last decade resulted in only some cosmetic changes around the operation of private pensions. The forty-five and ten vesting practice has been eliminated, pensions are more portable, and survival benefits at death and remarriage have been modified to reflect family patterns of the 1980s. It is all too easy to overdramatize the impact of these long overdue changes. But the most important outcome of the numerous studies and commissions is what *didn't* happen. Despite pressures from labour, women's, and pension reform groups, which included older people, there has been no expansion of the Canada Pension Plan. It still can only reflect 25 per cent of pensionable earnings. There has been no increase in the Old Age Security, which is the income floor for retired Canadians. The idea of a homemaker's pension received great media coverage but was never given serious political consideration.

Company-sponsored pensions are still not indexed to inflation. This means that pensioners' real incomes – the amount of real purchasing power per dollar – are whittled away as they get older. If the rate of inflation is 7 per cent per year, pensioners will have their retirement incomes roughly cut in half within a decade. In other words, the private pension industry was forced to clean up its act but there was no major policy shift. This means that those social forces behind today's poor old women and men will continue to oppress our children and grandchildren.

Government policy implicitly supports the stigmatization of poverty in the later years – this valuation of old people according to their past record – because it fails to provide the material support to enable old people to have the chance to lead decent lives. The poverty and inequality in society at large are reproduced and magnified in old age.

The Frustrations of
Easy Assumptions and False Images

Disability, it seems, works in many not-so-mysterious ways. In 1982, for instance, a friend and I chaired a symposium at the Canadian Association of Gerontology meeting in Winnipeg. Afterwards, feeling very good and positive about our work, Helen and I went off to enjoy the gala dinner that is usually a part of the CAG gathering.

Chatting away, we arrived at the pre-dinner reception and were greeted cheerily by a young man who gave us tickets for something. The music was loud so we did not hear exactly what he said. We both had hearing aids and they were no help in such a din because they amplify everything. We both wore glasses, but only for reading and we did not want to be bothered to get them out. We assumed (and I know that we should not assume anything, at least without glasses on) that we had been given bar tickets, and we made our way over to the bar quite unaware that the tickets in our hands were for a door prize.

The young man at the bar looked puzzled at the ticket my friend held out and explained very nicely that we had to buy bar tickets before we could get drinks. He pointed out where we had to go to do this. Off we went, feeling foolish. But more importantly, we felt sad that once again the image of old people as confused and having brain deterioration had probably been verified in the mind of that young man. In spite of the positive "Assets of Aging" theme of the conference, we ourselves had inadvertently added to the negative image of old people.

A simple mistake that could happen to anyone, certainly. But since we were in an age group already labelled negatively, the assumptions made about us would most likely increase the negative image. Not to hear and not to see – these are among the losses we are experiencing that have been called sensory deprivation. Sensory deprivation can have a devastating effect, as I well know from my own experience.

In fact, old people are not the only ones to be affected by such loss. Many younger people fall victim to the ever-increasing din of the workplace or the overuse of powerful sound systems developed with no thought for their potential damage. It is becoming more and more recognized that society needs to have better knowledge, be more aware of and sensitive to impaired hearing.

In May 1982 the Ontario Advisory Council on Senior Citizens issued a discussion paper on hearing impairment and the elderly.[13] The paper, prepared with the help of the Canadian Hearing Society, discussed the benefits of a highly mobile and industrialized society, and also its costs due to harmful changes in the environment. It recommended improved health care at the community level for older people with hearing problems. According to the paper, the major problem for old people who are hard of hearing is society's negative attitude to aging:

> If we assume hearing loss is simply a common occurrence of aging, then we will continue to ignore not only the problem but ways in which to assist this handicap. Hearing loss is not always manifested in recognizable ways, but rather may be gradual. The result is often withdrawal by the affected individual from society's mainstream. Lack of communication may result in many forms of deprivation, ranging from depression to loneliness.[14]

Time after time there are important meetings organized only for those who are able to hear, see, and move about freely. Even if there are ramps, amplifiers, and sign language in place, their availability is often not advertised or speakers fail to use the technology. A jaunty "everyone can hear *my* voice" and a sauntering back and forth across the stage spells doom for those seriously interested people who have some hearing loss. Their precious time and energy are squandered.

On one occasion, a highly successful centre for older people announced a public forum on an important and timely subject. A number of us welcomed the chance to be part of it, and travelled long distances to get there. Great pains had been taken by the centre people to provide adequate amplification for the large room. Their efforts were completely nullified by a cable TV crew, whose equipment caused a loud hum in opposition to the centre's system, no matter the attempted

adjustments. The TV crew should have known the arrange-
ment wouldn't work, but their goal was a good program for
their station that night. The TV people seemed to have no consideration for the disruption and disappointment of those in
attendance, and many of us left before the meeting was over –
having heard "nothing".

Then there was the time at my local supermarket, when I
witnessed an unfortunate but all too typical scene, the kind of
thing that more than anything else brings out my anger about
how old people in this society are treated. I was making slower
progress than usual along the rows of shelves, thanks to a problem with my back. But just ahead of me, pushing a big cart, was
a woman going even more slowly. Her progress was a kind of
shuffle on legs and feet that certainly were not in very good
shape for getting about. A man dropped something in her cart
and spoke to her. He seemed impatient, and hurried away and
then back to the cart again with another armful of purchases. I
realized he was in some way connected with the woman, a son,
a nephew, or neighbour perhaps. He was a well-dressed man
who seemed all in a rush to get back to the office or off to catch
a plane, or whatever. He kept pushing or pulling the cart,
depending on where he stood at any given time.

I ran into them again at the check-out counter. The man was
still there, obviously filled with anxiety at the slow process.
The young clerk went through the mechanics of checking the
groceries as quickly as possible, willingly listening to the old
woman's mumbled words and responding in a pleasant way to a
question about the Pope's visit. It was obvious the old woman
needed someone to talk to. For sure it would not be the man she
was with, at least not on this occasion. I could not resist
expressing my thanks to the check-out clerk for her perception
and helpful manner.

When I came home and sat down at my desk to do some
writing on the issue of aging, it really hit me that the old
woman and many others like her must feel like some kind of
fifth wheel – dragged along and taken care of with some reluc-
tance, not really considered necessary to the flow of things.

But what was also very apparent in this episode was the great difference between individual responses, and abilities to respond. There was the check-out girl who was patiently helpful, and the man who was with the old woman who could hardly spare the time. And I also had a glimpse, at the supermarket, of another woman I often see there doing her shopping by herself, a tiny, old Chinese woman in her eighties. She knows exactly what she wants to buy, knows the prices, and quickly sorts out the money, chatting with the checker all the time she does so. Although I'm not certain, I think she is the cultivator of a fine garden I see just down the street from my place. I see young people in this garden, too, but the old woman seems to be in command.

I wonder, what makes each of us so different? Is it cultural background, or our physical and mental well-being? Our life experiences? One thing is for sure: You can never say with any certainty that old people are any one thing or have any one particular set of characteristics. You cannot go ahead and set up a picture of a distinct and separate kind of being, a model for all of us.

The Challenge of Aging

Over the years I have watched and even been part of an explosion in the number of committees, agencies, research groups, government and non-government community services, projects, and a host of other undertakings all purportedly aimed at bettering the lives of older people. In spite of all these initiatives, the conditions of those in whose interest all this is being done have not improved very much. The "problem" of the elderly has been artificially created, the result too often of planning *for* old people, without input *from* them. In many cases, the needs of committees, agencies, and administration have taken priority over the needs of old people. In this way the supposed solutions have become part of the problem.

In spite of the high hopes that emerged from the watershed year of 1966, with the Senate Committee report, the first Canadian Conference on Aging, and a Canadian Social Welfare Council meeting highlighting aging, we still have negative stereotypes of old people in this country. Why do we continue to see old people as a monumental problem, one that is getting more acute as the years go by? How is it that, in spite of having poured such huge amounts of money, time, and effort into facilities for old people for two decades since that time, almost half of the people over sixty-five live below the poverty line? Why do our chances of being both poor and old increase if we are women? Why does every decent home for the aged or nursing home have a waiting list of a year or more? Why are active treatment beds in hospitals occupied by old people who don't need to be there? Something is very wrong.

Somehow, somewhere, society has gone off the rails in its treatment of old people.

In 1981 the National Advisory Council on Aging met to discuss priorities for action to tackle the most urgent problems facing elderly people in Canada. Heading the list was the need to transform the public perception of aging. Those who want to do the job of changing people's notions will have to be free of social prejudices against the old and will have to look forward towards their own aging in a positive manner.

> A better knowledge of aging, better information about the elderly, should make possible greater opportunities for this segment of the population. The later years of life, like any other, should be a time of growth, not of sadness. It is important for the public to regard these years as a period when intellectual, cognitive, affective and social development can be maintained and extended.[15]

Old age is just like childhood, youth, and middle age. It is part of the single thread that carries life through from the beginning, part of the natural progression of life. It has its challenges and difficulties just like any other part of life. One day a friend, Rudi, who was doing much thinking on these issues, scribbled out this message to me:

> Acceptance or respect cannot be demanded. Some people say it has to be earned. In fact, it comes naturally. To ask for accep-

tance, to ask for respect, becomes a senile act. The only way is to establish oneself, and acceptance and respect come normally. Old people should first of all change their attitude toward themselves. They should recognize the power they still have, both in their storage of knowledge and their physical strength. Then they must harness this power, united as a force that the society has to reckon with. The rest will come naturally.

One of our great challenges is to assume responsibility for ourselves and others to the limit of our capacity, on a day-to-day basis, regardless of age. By doing this we will come to understand the need for a lot more interdependence – as opposed to individualism. We need to help one another get around the barriers of age, gender, race, class, and all the other isolating factors in our lives.

My mother (left) holding my brother Lorne,
along with me and my brother John, at Riverside
Farm, in 1928.

3

From Growing Up
to Growing Old

This is where my world began. A world which includes
the ancestors – both my own and other peoples' ancestors
who became mine. A world which formed me, and continues to do so, even while I fought it in some of its
aspects, and continue to do so. A world which gave me my
own lifework to do, because it was here that I learned the
sight of my own particular years.

MARGARET LAURENCE, *Heart of a Stranger*

I PUT THE LETTER down. The white-haired, bright-eyed old
gentleman I had known as Grandpa was dead.

Too late now to continue my questioning about Cromarty
County in the north-western highlands of Scotland, where he
was born. Too late to find out more about life in Mount Forest,
Ontario, where he had grown up. Now I'd have to ask someone
else about the move to southwestern Manitoba and the estab-
lishment of the farm in 1886. My family called it Riverside

Farm, and it was close to the town of Killarney. That's where I grew up.

I looked at the letter again. Then, amidst the rich quiet of the northern muskeg, far from my family and our home, I began to think about times that I associated with life then and with my grandfather: Sunday evenings around the piano or organ, visits from my father's cousins who lived seventy-five miles away in Brandon. It was from family members that I learned the bits and pieces of the story of how my grandfather, George McCulloch, settled in Manitoba and built the large frame house we lived in, about witching for water or losing one of the horses in a spring flood.

At the time my grandfather died I was living in Northern Manitoba at Norway House, teaching in the Indian Residential School. Perhaps this experience caused me to reflect on my own family background. As I got to know something of the lives of the Native girls and boys and their parents and grandparents, I was able to better appreciate the values that governed their society. Everyone – young and old – was important and would always be cared for in some family, whether they were related or not. The very closeness of Indian people to one another made me aware of how far away my own people were and how very little I knew about my own roots. The people I was living among were linked to their past through the land and a complex of legends recounted by the elders. As I read the letter telling me of my grandfather's death, I realized how cut off my society was becoming from its own past.

Certainly, I had tried to piece together as much of my family's history as I could. I knew that both sides of my family came to Manitoba as part of the settler wave of Scots and Irish whose first stopping point had been Ontario or Quebec. I knew that they had helped build up the community where I was born, a community that was mostly British and English-speaking. But I grew up unaware of the rich cultural heritage surrounding our farm. The Scottish and Irish immigrants, some of whom only spoke the Gaelic, shared the new territory with an existing French-speaking community and a Native society for whom the land was not new at all. Still later, immigrants from

Central Europe moved into the province. And yet, to me all of these others were invisible.

Farm Life – For Young and Old

I was the oldest of a large family and this may have had something to do with being shut off from other lifestyles. At a time when the economy was worsening after the boom of the gay nineties and the beginning of the twentieth century, just to keep family and farm afloat meant little time for anything else. I remember how I burst into tears when I heard that my mother had just given birth to her eighth child. The aunt who passed on the news tried to comfort me. "There, there now. They're both fine." But I wasn't crying out of my concern for my mother and her new son. At sixteen, I was tired of babies and resented my mother for having yet another.

Those years were very confusing for me. I loved the country life and the farm. I knew my parents were doing their utmost to give us children a good life in a community they were helping to shape. But so often the Herculean effort went for nothing. The money from the harvest had to go to the mortgage company and the family went without. A community project failed because people didn't want an increase in taxes, even if the undertaking promised to make the community a better place to live. I was constantly torn between questioning why this should be and accepting the hopes of my parents that things would be better if only we kept on working hard.

Even at a young age, these seeming injustices bothered me, and I would have dearly loved to discuss them with my parents. But the very real business of life kept us fully occupied. There were ten or more people to be fed three times a day, clothes to be washed, ironed, and mended, a house to be cleaned. There were cows to be milked, poultry and small animals to be tended, a garden to be planted, weeded, and harvested. There were fruit preserves to prepare, wood to be gathered, sick children to be cared for. There was attendance at school – a very important matter in our family – with its own activities for all of us. All this did not allow much time for heart-to-heart communication.

Still, there were compensations. Today, when grandparents and grandchildren sometimes hardly ever see each other, to look back is to realize how fortunate we were to have known all four of our grandparents and two of our great-grandparents. My maternal grandparents lived in a nearby town and there were regular trips back and forth. Every member of our family visited this old couple on many occasions. We'd bring farm-fresh eggs, butter, milk and cream for them. At their place there was always something to eat after the long ride in from the farm. There was a warm place by the stove in winter, a shady hammock in summer.

Although they were no longer in their original location on the farm, Grandpa still maintained a large garden for vegetables and an orchard with about a dozen different kinds of small fruit trees. With gardening in the summer and curling in the winter, he had plenty to do as he grew older. Sometimes, at harvest time, he would come to our farm to drive us to school. No one else was able to "spare" the time. For Grandma there was never an idle moment. She preserved, canned, and pickled most of the produce from the garden. She also had a couple of business ventures – a knitting machine and a corsetier's agency – to provide her with a little money of her own.

Grandpa and Grandma, who both lived into their early seventies, were busy people as they lived out their lives among family and friends. They never did see themselves, nor did the rest of the family see them, as "senior citizens", a people set apart. They were industrious, independent old people involved with things that were going on around them.

Community life was stitched together by the institutions of church and school and by special events like Christmas, school field days, agricultural fairs, and Chautauqua, a travelling show that brought educational and cultural events from other parts of the world to rural Canada.

Only now, in retrospect, do I realize how important a role women like my mother and the others of her generation played in Canadian life in the early part of the twentieth century.

Much of their effort was channelled through the Federated Women's Institutes of Canada, started in 1897 by Adelaide Hunter Hoodless. The Women's Institute supported equal pay for equal work as early as 1919 and published a booklet in 1921 on the legal status of women in Canada. The Women's Institute was late in coming to our district but Mother felt it was important because it attempted to link women and children everywhere. The WI was and still is affiliated with another organization, the Association of Country Women of the World, which today has over nine million members in sixty-two countries around the world.[1] The ACWW aims to help rural women use all the resources they can muster to improve conditions for their families and themselves.

Years after I left Manitoba I visited a rural women's sewing group in Ghana, part of a community project to improve living conditions. I was amazed to see a piece of coarse cotton with "Lake of the Woods Milling Company" stamped in one corner. One of the African women explained, through an interpreter, that she could not get those letters off no matter what she did. When I heard that, my mind did a quick flip back to dry, dusty days on the farm in Manitoba and Grandma saying the very same thing about the very same kind of coarse cotton flour bags from that same milling company. Time, distance, and differences melted away as I thought about women and their efforts to provide for their children in whatever way possible.

In our community, members of mother's Women's Institute group decided to make life a little less difficult for rural families by securing a site and a building that they could furnish and operate as a rest-room in town. The completion of the project was a real blessing and an eye-opener to the community. It proved what women could do. It also gave women visiting town a measure of independence as well as a place to relax and rest.

Providing a rest-room involved the whole community, and the co-operation seemed to help bridge the differences that I was beginning to see in the society around me, gaps between rich and poor, between town and country, and between men and women. Looking back, I realize I felt these differences very keenly indeed. But although I may have felt them, I had no way of airing my concerns. The training of the times was towards acceptance and doing as we were told.

Fred Grayston, a "senior activist" in Vancouver, says that most old people don't get involved in political issues because they "have an ingrained fear of authority".[2] I have often wondered if that is why so many of us who are now old have not questioned a system which has lumped us together and designated us as senior citizens.

Certainly, the social, political, and technological changes that formed the backdrop of my early years all had an effect on the status of older people in society. World War I, the rapid growth of cities and industry, even so apparently beneficial a change as increasing electrification of farm life, all had far-reaching consequences.

The trend to urbanization had its strong effect even in the country, with the coming of the car and the radio, more and better roads, greater access to consumer services. More and more commercial companies began to offer canned fruits and vegetables in varying size, quality, and price. For busy farmers, into ever-growing wheat acreage, it was much easier and less time-consuming to buy canned goods than to plant, tend, and preserve products in gardens of their own. The gathering and preparation of vegetables was taken out of the hands of those who had felt themselves to be contributing to the family well-being by performing these tasks. The coming of electricity did away with a number of the chores that an old person might have done, like churning, pumping water, caring for small animals, and the like. In the city some chores old people used to do became unnecessary due to the closeness of a corner store or, later, a supermarket. Children could now get to school on their own.

There were other changes as well. The "scientific" care of babies tended to make grandma and the rocking chair obsolete, at least for a few decades. In smaller city houses where there didn't seem to be nearly so much that needed doing, older family members quickly sensed that there was no longer a place for them, even though this question was seldom raised in the family circle. Old people started to feel trapped. To get money from the government felt like charity, especially to those who had for so long valued their independence and self-reliance. They had always paid their own way, gone without, or been in debt to the bank. It was hard for them to accept that they had a right, through the taxes they had paid, to the small sums of pension money that the government provided for their welfare.

That same sense of independence in old people kindled anxiety over the prospects of becoming a burden on their children. What to do? Many accepted what seemed inevitable and became, ever so unwillingly, senior citizens.

Anthropology and the Mode of Production

I frequently get a bit overwhelmed by the amount of depressing news I receive about aging. This is all too often reflected in my own writing. The same pejorative adjectives keep popping up: poor; dependent; separate; useless. But I'm not being a naysayer. I'm simply relaying the messages that I receive along with everyone else who reads a paper or watches TV.

On the front page of the newspaper one day I saw one of those little items editors include as "human interest" in order to leaven the matters of great social and political import cramming their columns. The inch-long story was headlined "Man Seeks Place in Sands of Time". It concerned a sixty-two-year-old unemployed Englishman from Bristol who wanted to have his ashes placed in an egg-timer when he died. He was going to bequeath the egg-timer to his daughter because he had nothing else to leave her. "Because of my bad legs I cannot work any more," he explained. "But one day I shall be of some use again."

This kind of anecdote tends to make me look back to the past, to a time when old people like my grandparents had useful roles to play. Living in a small town near our farm, integrated into family life, they could still participate. This is how I had seen older people when I was a young child, so it's tempting to idealize that situation and look back with nostalgia to the good old days.

Many of us, confronted with overwhelming evidence about the plight of old people in industrial society, also sometimes romanticize the position of the elderly in pre-industrial times, when things were simpler. Such societies maintained close kinship and family networks. Local communities were more stable than in present-day Canada and society was generally characterized by more reciprocity and mutual dependence. But simply because a society is not industrialized does not mean that old people will, by definition, be well-treated.

In her book *Old Age* Simone de Beauvoir provides a survey of the status and fate of old people in dozens of different societies. She finds that the treatment of old people varies tremendously, often according to the level of material security in society. A group of semi-nomadic Siberian people, the Yakuts, lived in a land where many suffered from hunger and deprivation. The climate was harsh, and families were organized along patriarchal lines. The father owned the livestock that represented wealth, and had absolute authority. He could sell off or kill disobedient children, or simply disinherit them. But when a man declined with age, his sons were likely to turn on him, take his possessions, and either let him die or abuse him as they had been abused themselves. Many old people, both men and women, starved. Simone de Beauvoir writes, "Extreme shortage of food, a low cultural level and the hatred of the parents bred by patriarchal harshness – everything conspired against the old."[3]

In contrast, a group of native people in Brazil, the Jivaro, had a relatively prosperous society. They lived from hunting, gathering, and agriculture in the rain forest of the Amazon basin. The elderly men were respected, as their knowledge of the jungle gave rise to pharmacology and the other uses of the thousands of plants and animals that populate the forest environment. The elderly also passed along stories and songs from their forebears, thus preserving social continuity. Part of the religious belief of the Jivaro was that, if the old were ill-treated, they could be born again in the form of a dangerous animal like a snake or a jaguar and return to avenge past cruelties.[4]

The evidence of the anthropologists and ethnologists provides a variety of comparisons of the treatment of old people in different times and places. Against this background it becomes difficult to generalize about the old being better off in pre-industrial societies. However, an important variable that has characterized many societies is the relationship old people have with the way of making a living, the mode of production.

Throughout history and in many places people continued to own or control their tools and their craft skills well into what was considered old age. When they got old this control allowed them to decide for themselves to what extent they would continue to work. Since work was frequently carried out within the family and the family was the primary unit of production, continuity was easier to achieve. In agricultural societies where ownership of the land is crucial in determining power and status, old farmers who maintain control of the land will not likely be ignored, cast aside, or despised.

My parents were born into a society that was agricultural and shared many of the characteristics of the pre-industrial situation. Farmers and craft workers are independent producers who can control their participation in the economy, timing their withdrawal and perhaps doing a little bit here, a little bit there, right up until that time when they can work no longer. Business, trade, and commerce rested largely in the hands of small merchants who related to work and production in the same way.

In Canada today most old people have no ownership or control over the means of production. In fact, many people have only their own labour power to sell in order to make a living.

Ultimate control over the economy has shifted from small producers to large corporations that control most of the wealth. Huge government agencies regulate and mediate many aspects of our lives. Such big outfits operate for the most part according to strict bureaucratic guidelines. Gone are the days when most people could pace their own withdrawal from work and productive activity. One analysis of aging in pre-industrial societies concludes:

> Whenever the existing property of a society becomes concentrated into the hands of a very small proportion of the population, and without adequate means of redistribution, its effectiveness as a means of participation for the majority of people is

greatly diminished. If concentration of property ownership is carried too far, large numbers of old people will become dependent in an otherwise rich society.[5]

When people are forced out of the labour market by retirement or infirmity their chances of doing well in material terms plummet. Since a person's value is so closely bound up with what they do – or do not do – the esteem they command also declines when they get old and stop working. This is a situation many old people like myself face every day.

Training and Jobs and Other Changes

My own early life was in no way exempt from the effects of the changes in society. If my parents and grandparents made up a Pioneer Generation, I guess I was part of the so-called Depression Generation. We were born around the time of World War I, grew up during what was for some the heady boom period of the 1920s, and came down to earth with a thud when the Depression hit in 1929. Moreover, those of us raised on prairie farms can well recall nature's contribution to those dark days, when drought ravaged the land. It was a difficult time for a young person starting out in life. Unemployment was rampant and people lost self-confidence as their talents and skills had no apparent application.

My own route towards a job was circuitous. Towards the end of high school the minister of our combination schoolhouse-church asked me to be a delegate to a young people's convention in Brandon. I was surprised, because up until then I had shown little, if any, interest in church matters. But I went anyway and became part of a group of rural young people who attended a World Sunday School convention in Toronto in 1930.

This experience opened up new horizons and seemed to offer a way I could shape my life. It awakened a kind of awareness – a potential of mind and spirit – that I had sensed in my parents and some other people I knew, but that I had not found in school, church, or community institutions until then. It impressed me deeply to be part of a world gathering of people from various backgrounds and cultures, people who spoke different languages and dressed in different ways, but who all shared a common belief in Christianity. I felt that I wanted to remain part of that fellowship. When I came back from Toronto I entered church-organized work with young people with such zeal that my brothers teasingly changed my nickname from Fatty to Aimee, after the American evangelist Aimee Semple McPherson.

My involvement with young people included organizing local groups, co-ordinating them with provincial and national groupings, as well as organizing summer camps with a religious orientation. This experience led me to embark at age twenty on two years of training to be a deaconess, a church-woman who works as a kind of assistant to the male clergy. This meant a rigorous program of study at United Colleges, now the University of Winnipeg.

The deaconess course involved classes with young men training to be ministers. I and another young woman were the only females in the group, although one of the professors was also a woman. Here the divisions I had been seeing in relationships in my home community came into sharp relief. To my feelings about the differences in status between town and country and rich and poor was now added a sense of similar differences between the sexes. Looking back, I realize that on many occasions I felt patronized by the male theology students and even some female students in other faculties. I was, after all, a girl fresh from the farm trying to learn the right way to go about life in the city and at the same time handle all the work involved at the college. I was expected to be pleasant and charming with all those around me.

At the time I didn't challenge the men or their attitudes. To do so would have been totally unacceptable behaviour on the part of a young girl. In the shared training, any concern with social issues extended only as far as lectures on the value of milk for the "needy".

A few men in our graduating class, however, were very much aware of the need for new political dimensions and became members of the then-new CCF (Co-operative Commonwealth Federation), in which they worked ardently for social change. Two of them, Stanley Knowles and Lloyd Stinson, later became federal members of parliament. Another organization, the Student Christian Movement, also helped to bring social concerns onto the campus. I met my future husband, George Marshall, among this interested group of students.

Although I was uneasy about it, the theological courses and the required fieldwork kept me busy and there was little time provided and still less incentive to think about the broader issues of the depression and social conditions. There were no jobs for young people and we were living in a city where most people had very little money. Looking back I realize that during my deaconness training course we were isolated from the real world around us.

I was offered a job after graduation but my family's need for my help at home was so pressing that I knew I had to turn it down and return to Riverside Farm. Those were difficult times for me. I felt very much alone as I pondered what was ahead in my life. Certainly my help on the farm would be needed and appreciated for the next while, but my contacts in the church were placing strong and vocal pressures on me to follow up my training. After a time, when an invitation came for me to teach the Bible study course in a nearby church leadership summer camp, I decided to accept. A little later I was asked to conduct a church vacation school program in a Winnipeg church. In both cases the church covered my expenses but offered no salary.

These experiences were stimulating enough to make me feel I had made the right decision and that soon there *would* come the offer of paid work, which I had to have unless I returned home again.

A paid job did appear, rather unexpectedly. Before I knew it, I was on my way to the Indian Residential School at Norway House in Northern Manitoba to be sewing-room supervisor and music teacher. At first I argued that I was not even qualified to teach these subjects, but I was assured that my most important qualification was my Christian commitment. On that basis, off I went. I had no knowledge at all of the people or the society I would encounter when I arrived, and now I was going to be living and working among them, supposedly in a leadership capacity.

In the area around Norway House Native people were still carrying on their traditional subsistence activities, hunting and fishing. There was trapping, as well, since furs could be sold to a local trader. But this work could not support the people in the area. Indian society was in the process of being wrenched apart by the impact of white culture and white domination.

The churches were right in there, running residential schools paid for mostly by the government. The church was responsible for staff and curriculum and there was competition between churches for students, because the government subsidy increased as enrolment grew. Mighty promises were extended to parents in a bid to attract their children to one school or another. I knew nothing of all this when I arrived, filled with the desire to do good work for these "poor Indian children".

I spent four years at Norway House in jobs that were unrelated to my formal training. I was in charge of the sewing room and helped the teacher with music in the classroom. At regular times each week I took my turn at supervision of the kitchen, laundry, recreation periods inside and out, and daily walks. Unexpectedly, in my last year at the school I found myself in charge of the kitchen instead of being responsible for music and play for the pre-school children as planned.

After only a short time in the community I learned that Indian people had their own unique concept of family and community relationships. Indian parents were closely attached to their children and only tolerated sending them away to residential school for most of the year because they thought the schooling would help the children out in later life.

I can still feel the pathos of seeing five-year-old twin girls sitting on their father's knees in the principal's office. The father knew he had to leave them in a few hours and from his troubled expression I could tell how uneasy and full of doubts he was. Only his great respect for the principal, Rev. Roscoe Chapin, who had previously been a missionary on his reserve, made it possible for the father to leave his girls with us.

This father's doubts proved to be well-founded. It was some

time before any of us realized that while the Indian children were kept warm and well fed, they weren't getting an appropriate education. They were left both ill-equipped for life in white society and untrained in the traditional skills required for life on the reserve.

I left Norway House in 1938, when, in spite of my somewhat tarnished image of ministers-in-training, I married one fresh out of theological college. I began a new phase of my life, as George Marshall's wife in The Pas, Manitoba.

I soon found that the role of "wife of the minister" was not only very public but also very restricted. The seeds of future doubt, I think, were sown during those early years. I often sat in the choir or the congregation listening raptly to George preach. I wondered how people could ignore the meaning of what he was saying, its relevance to our lives. He discussed with depth and sincerity the Christian beliefs that were so much a part of his life. As he pointed out, the Christian faith had not been tried and found wanting, it simply hadn't been tried, and the truth of the statement seemed very clear from where I sat. But each Sunday there would be the same ritual handshake and pat on the back at the church door as all of us went out to plan for the next week in just the same way as we had before. From what I could see, there seemed to be little serious consideration of what had been said.

I also had to deal with other changes, even more difficult. Only a year after our marriage, my grandmother took sick. Despite the devoted care of my mother and a nurse, Grandmother died, in her own home, soon after. Only a few weeks later my mother was suddenly rushed by ambulance to the hospital in Brandon, where she herself died within a few hours. I went home for her funeral but I could only stay for a short while, because I had a separate life now. Leaving home this time was the hardest of all. It was agonizing to say goodbye to my grieving father and the rest of the family, but there was no choice.

While travelling home on the bus I realized that I was pregnant. The changes kept coming, some tragic, some joyful. Our family was not unique. What happened to us was happening, and will continue to happen, to families everywhere as generations come and go.

*   *

The birth of my three daughters, our family's moves to other pastorates in Boissevain and Winnipeg, the daily round of seemingly endless obligations, all of these things absorbed my time and energy for over two decades. Then suddenly all of this was in the past. George became ill with what at first seemed to be pneumonia but which led to the discovery of lung cancer and the need for immediate surgery. At first he went through a slow, successful recovery and was able to go back to his ministry for six months. Then another period of ill health followed until finally – despite his own valiant efforts to recover, and all the concerned care he got from those around him – death claimed George at age forty-eight.

In January 1959, after twenty years of being a minister's wife I became a minister's widow with three children, no home, and little money. There was also no work in sight that I could use to support myself and help my daughters continue the kind of education we had hoped they would want. It is surprising how quickly things can change. Within a short time I was working with the community service committee in a large inner-city United church.

All of a sudden I was involved in the organization of a noon-time hot meal and after-school care program for the children of working mothers. I was also in charge of setting up a program for older people in the community. Ever since that time, a period of almost thirty years, my work has centred on the position of old people in Canada and now my own old age has been deeply affected by what I have learned over the past three decades.

The Sunshine Club's orchestra in Winnipeg in the early sixties.

4

Caring and Retirement:
The Rites of Passage

It is the meaning that men attribute to their life, it is their entire system of values that define the meaning and value of old age. The reverse applies: by the way in which a society behaves towards its old people it uncovers the naked, and often carefully-hidden, truth about its real principles and aims.

SIMONE DE BEAUVOIR, *Old Age*

THE TWENTY-FIVE years following the end of World War Two were really the golden age for the institution of retirement. People like myself taught "preparation for retirement" courses. There was an explosion in the growth of private and public pension plans. Programs for retired people proliferated as groups with names like The Harvest Years Association and the Busy Oldsters Club got started. The business of homes for the aged got going in a big way as various Lodges and Manors appeared as if out of nowhere. I always got a kick out of attempts to give such places appropriate names, but my favorites remain Sunset Lodge and – best of all – the Golden Stairs Nursing Home.

Aging was a new field in Canada when I formally entered it in the 1950s. Indeed, aging had never before been a distinct discipline, something to be studied and assessed. Gerontology was nudging its way into the academic world to take its place among the respected social sciences like sociology and anthropology. While I was busy learning, making mistakes, and being forced to challenge my assumptions about aging during the period of my work with the United Church, theorists across North America were busily developing explanations as to why so many old people were separated from society. Before my eyes legions of social workers, including people like myself, started to plan activities for old people outside the context of a paid job.

Out of this new interest in aging emerged something called "disengagement theory". A Canadian textbook on aging summarizes disengagement theory:

> Because of the inevitability of death, because of the probable decrement in ability as one ages, because of the value placed on youth, and because of the need to ensure that tasks are efficiently completed and roles filled, both individuals and society demand disengagement ... normal aging is viewed as a functional and voluntary process that involves the inevitable withdrawal or disengagement of the individual from society and of society from the individual.[1]

It all seemed neat and simple. But I only had to think back to how "engaged" people like my grandparents had been as they kept on contributing to family life, the family farm, and to society at large. This made me wonder about the seeming inevitability of disengagement. How did this fit in with the disengagement theories of the new gerontologists? What had happened to make disengagement possible?

Jessica's Retirement Home

A friend of mine, Jessica, provides a perfect example of someone who resisted the heavy push towards disengagement.

When I first met Jessica, it was like meeting someone I had already known for years; I had heard so much about her. She was a "professional" social worker held in high regard by those who worked with her; I was a "paraprofessional" working in the field of aging. And indeed, when we met we had a lot in common. An hour or two together revealed that much of our experience in the work we had done, most of our perceptions of what was happening to old people, were the same.

At the time we first met Jessica was exploring the possibilities of moving into a "retirement home". It happened that we had both read an advertisement for such a home: "Retirement at its finest. If you are fifty-five years or older and can *manage on your own* we more than welcome you to our Home." It seemed everything one could hope for, "centrally located, reasonably priced". Just the thing, thought Jessica. Lately she had toyed with the idea of a change in her living arrangements. The very large apartment where she then lived was beginning to take more time and energy – and rental income – than she wanted to give to it.

Jessica told me that after she saw the ad she took her time thinking things over and talking with her family. "Finally," she said, "I decided to go and see what it was like. Much of what I saw I liked. But I still wanted more time before making such a big change."

Finally Jessica did apply for admission and, as she said, "began to plan my life accordingly". She was assured by the people she talked to at the home that she could bring along some of her own furniture – anything except her bed. So she began to think about what to take and how to arrange it in the small space that would be her home.

"The more I thought about it the less I liked the idea. I couldn't sleep at night. I began to have difficulty with meals, because I couldn't seem to digest food properly – I guess I was getting so nervous. But I reasoned with myself that I must go ahead and get ready to move – and that I'd best get on with it."

Jessica got her nephew to go with her to measure the room and help her decide what to take. But when she asked someone at the home if she could see the room and take some measurements, this person – whom she hadn't seen on her previous visit – said, rather impatiently, "There's no point in doing that. We don't allow anyone to bring along their furniture, you know." Jessica didn't *know* that. Later she said to me, "Such a statement was in direct contradiction to what I'd been told a few months earlier. I was angry and said so."

The experience made Jessica more than a little suspicious of the retirement home and she began to mull over the prospects. She said her anger helped to clear her mind. "I began to realize," she said, "that taking or leaving my furniture was not in itself at the root of my unease and loss of sleep. Rather, it was a growing doubt about whether or not I could live out my life in an environment controlled by influences outside myself – about which the issue of 'furniture' had been significantly revealing."

Shortly after, she found out that there was a forthcoming vacancy for a smaller apartment in her own building. She discussed with her nephew the option of managing in a smaller place and whether she could continue to stay in her present apartment until the smaller one was available. She talked with friends who had already taken up residence in a retirement home. She found that some were pleased, some were sorry. She was still uncertain about what to do. When she phoned her nephew he told her, "You're the only one who can make the choice, Jessica. Whatever you decide, we'll try our best to help you."

She knew her nephew was right, and finally made the decision. "I would stay in my big place until the smaller apartment was open for rental. Needless to say, the retirement-home people weren't happy when I cancelled out. But I had a good sleep and meals were a pleasure again."

When Jessica told me about all this – over a long cup of tea one afternoon – I couldn't help but admire her careful decision, which for her seemed so ideal. To help her continue living at the apartment building she had arranged for a grocer to deliver her telephoned orders. She had found someone to do the heavy cleaning and had made other convenient arrangements for services such as laundry, drycleaning, and orders from the liquor store. And now there we were, enjoying tea together in her pleasant apartment. It was smaller, of course, than she had ever realized; much of her furniture had had to go. She had been forced to make adjustments to a worsening physical capability. But most importantly she had an essential feeling of control over her own life, as always.

"I know I may have to move sometime, but I'm so glad that I decided to stay for the time being," Jessica said. Although I did not say so I felt glad, too, that for this woman, at least, such a decision had been possible.

Working With Older People in Winnipeg

My personal experience with the politics of retirement and disengagement started in the late 1950s when, shortly after the death of my husband, I started my job as staff person for the community service committee in a Winnipeg United Church. The job included, among other things, a program to improve life for older people in the community.

One of my tasks was visiting older people in various health care facilities – hospitals or nursing homes, for the most part – around the city, and in doing this I began to discover great differences, both in the facilities themselves and in the people I found there, residents and staff alike. Some of my visits were pleasant, such as time spent with someone in a well-run, huge old house renovated to provide living space for those who could afford to be looked after in a decent manner. The place was well-run and "homey" in the real sense of the word. There were tea parties almost every afternoon, attended by friends who dropped by with flowers, sweets, and gifts as well as all the latest gossip about family and friends.

In another facility, larger and more like a hospital, I visited an old man, a former logger who was bedridden and nearly impossible to reach in any human way. A staff member told me he had been there for several years and that no relative or friend had ever visited, written, or phoned. I started to come regularly, each time bringing a small gift. Although he rarely said a word, when he heard my voice he would always reach out his hand for the chocolate bar provided by the "visiting shut-ins fund" of the church. I was very impressed by the real feelings of concern shown for him by staff people in that rather barren place.

The worst visits on my schedule took me to people who had become utterly confused and were unable to remain at home. I visited one woman in a large old house that had been converted into an institution for the elderly. The place was overcrowded, with every inch of space used to house more people than it could possibly accommodate. When I went in, the woman I was visiting would be in a room with several other women, each in some stage of undress, unable to recognize friends or relatives. She was just sitting there looking at the world over the bottom of a locked half-door. The scene always reminded me of the stable for our animals back home on the farm. But our stable had seemed warm, clean, and somehow inviting. The same could not be said for this place where people had been filed away to live out their days.

Although such situations shocked me each time I confronted them, there seemed little to be done for the people living in such a condition. I knew that in Winnipeg work was being carried out to establish standards, safety regulations, adequate space, sufficient staff, and nutritious meals, all in order to provide better care in small and large settings for old people in nursing homes. But even now, in many places and many years later, the same kinds of shocking situations still exist, despite more knowledge of and, in some instances, greater effort to help. Sometimes there are standards in place, sometimes not. But no matter how high the standard, now more than ever I am convinced that legislation alone is not enough to ensure humane use of a nursing home facility.

The Sunshine Club

One of the first things our committee did in Winnipeg in order to come closer to meeting the needs of old people was to set up an afternoon recreational program for older people living in their own homes around the church.

The notion proved to be a good one. The Sunshine Club – the name chosen by the participants – made a real difference in the lives of the men and women, many in their eighties, who came every week to a gathering place in the church. The space was used in a variety of ways, friendships developed, and skills were used to the extent that each could contribute. Often the post-man or delivery people would stop and listen to the sound of music, dancing, and cheery greeting as they opened the door off the hall to catch a glimpse of the scene inside. There were times of quiet, too, as news of someone who was sick or the death of a member, sometimes more than one, was shared and sympathy extended.

A description of the program appeared in a presentation to the Manitoba Conference of the United Church:

> To come to the large church hall any Friday now is to find one-self in an atmosphere of warmth and friendliness – one has a quiet feeling of being part of something vital and meaningful. It's the Sunshine Club and the people who come chose the name. Most of them are 75-85 years old, a bit hard to believe, of course, if you happen to arrive as a few couples are enjoying a little waltz. The music is supplied by our violinist, who is 82, or the accordionist, who is 76 ... only two of the people who contribute items for the enjoyment of all.

The emphasis of the Sunshine Club was on providing the means whereby physically able older people could participate in activities similar to those they had known in their home communities in the small town or on farms in Manitoba. There, they had no trouble keeping busy doing things like plan-ning and carrying out meetings with church and / or commun-ity groups, or serving refreshments at the local rink or the sum-mer fair to raise money for worthy causes. They would visit hospitals or homes when sickness had overtaken a friend or family member, and go to funerals, weddings, or other gather-ings. And there were social times – a community dance, concert, ballgame, curling banquet – that had to be squeezed into their already full routine.

Looking back I can see that providing the space and support for the Sunshine Club to grow was really setting the stage for a new community to evolve, giving displaced old people a chance to come alive as they resumed parts of their former routine of involvement.

But it wasn't long before we realized that the club was not the answer for some old people in the neighbourhood – those who were still living in their own homes or apartments with help from family or friends. We decided to offer a home-cooked meal at the church once a week and if needed to provide transportation to the meals. There would be time for visiting and socializing following the meal. We worked with other social agencies in the community, with our congregation, with doctors, and with people's families to find out who might want and need this service.

This pilot project was a real blessing for those who used it, but unfortunately its life was brief. Thought to be "too much for too few", it was terminated after a highly successful Christmas dinner at the end of a three-month trial.

One of those who had taken meals with the project was my Great-Aunt Lolla, exactly one hundred years old and almost totally blind. Her nieces and nephews lived nearby and helped her with shopping and meals on a daily basis. They might bring her a meal or have one sent by taxi. Sometimes they would take her out for dinner, although she hated to go out for a meal because she found restaurant portions too large to eat and disliked the thought of wasting any food. For Aunt Lolla, the once-a-week meal program was ideal. It allowed her to get out and mingle with people and at the same time have a meal suited to her needs.

I have good memories of her at that final Christmas dinner, in itself perfect, complete with a beautifully roasted turkey carved at the table by one of the participants. Knowing how poor Aunt Lolla's eyesight was, it was with a sense of pleasurable awe that I saw her sitting straight as a ramrod (she was an ultracorrect Englishwoman), managing her cutlery with precision so that every scrap of food was eaten with restrained but evident enjoyment. After the meal the group wanted to sing Christmas carols, so I asked Aunt Lolla if she would play the piano for us. She had been a music teacher, but was initially a bit hesitant. We helped her to the piano, and as soon as her fingers felt the keys the hesitancy evaporated and she played for half an hour while the group sang along. That's how I remember her – sitting up straight as a pole, relaxed and happy doing something she loved with others around her who appreciated her skill.

The Not-So-Golden Age of Retirement

My work with old people in the 1950s made me aware of the particular kind of attention being paid to the men and women who were retiring and the new problems they were facing. It was at this time that the concept of "senior citizen" became firmly established and periodicals aimed specifically at old people began to appear. I got the sense that aging was an issue whose time had come when *Senior Citizen* and *Modern Maturity* began to appear on the newsstands. At a time when government spending on social services was expanding, old people became the targets of the ministrations of social workers.

This is not to say that some of them were not in need; everyone needs some kind of help sometimes – the later years are certainly no exception. People will always need help as they get on in years. But, from what I could see, the dominant approach to aging taken by social workers and gerontologists centred on the needs of old people *outside* the job.

I have only to look back to my years in church programs like the Sunshine Club to realize how our efforts were geared towards providing old people with *something to do* – a focus for their lives. Social activity was seen to be the answer to the problems of the elderly and too few of us made the connection between these problems and the fact that many people had been forced into idleness. Their dilemma had been socially produced, the result of them being forced to make a sudden break with their former occupations and ways of life.

There were powerful forces backing the institution of mandatory retirement and they added their voices to the chorus singing the praises of life in the golden years. Esso said that "retirement is something earned by faithful service, a form of 'graduation' into a new phase of life rather than a 'casting out' process".[2] Given the "set" of society and *no* preparation for using retirement years, the "casting out" remained the central factor in the minds and hearts of the retired no matter what anyone said.

When I looked around at the old people in the church hall, at the Sunshine Club, I realized that I was helping to plan programs with them precisely because they were outside the mainstream of society. They did not appear to be fully engaged. Why?

In the new world of consumerism with its built-in obsolescence, the "throw away and buy new" concept was carried over into the realm of people – those who produced and those who did not. Old people were clearly in the second category. It all seemed to have something to do with retirement and the notion that there came a time in your life when you stopped what you were doing and either did something else or did nothing at all. In the midst of the post-war boom a consumer society and retirement became normal. What's more, retirement was usually mandatory.

Retirement was not something that developed magically, unrelated to changes in society. It was the response of the managers of society in government and business to the needs of a changing economy. Around the time I was born, Eastern Canada was undergoing a profound change. Small, family-owned businesses were starting to be replaced by larger corporations. The expanding automotive and electrical industries were dominated by a few large firms. In my lifetime some farms, like ours, acquired Massey-Harris machinery. Companies like Ford, General Electric, and Westinghouse became household names as consumer goods became much more widely available than ever before. Money to purchase these commodities was another matter.

The era of big business was the era of progress, efficiency, and industrial expansion. Managers sought ways of increasing productivity by bringing in new machines. As mechanical complexity increased, experience in the ways of the past was invalidated. Management claimed to be basing decisions on science and the growth of this scientific management accompanied the expansion of factories and the introduction of the assembly line. Work became intense, pressure-ridden.

Workers, like the machines they operated, could become worn out and no longer able to produce satisfactorily. "Most employers regretfully acknowledge," said a banker at the time, "that it takes but a few years to use up a worker, so high is the pace at which work is now done. The employer is not to blame. He must keep his output up to the mark or be forced to the wall."[3]

What to do with the people who had been doing the labour, who were inevitably slowing down, who were having trouble adapting to the new ways?

Retirement helped to solve this problem. By establishing an age at which employees *had* to leave the job, it freed managers in the new industrial bureaucracies from the obligations of the past. Everyone had to retire; therefore the system would be treating everyone equally. Personnel departments within administrative hierarchies were, if anything, impersonal. They followed a set of guidelines laid down as part of company policy – the gold watch syndrome.

Whereas the old-fashioned owner-manager might feel vulnerable to a plea from an older worker to be allowed to stay on the job, the new style of bureaucratic manager could simply shrug and say, "I'm sorry, Mr. West, it's a matter of company policy. I don't make the rules, I just work here. And besides, if we made an exception in your case, we'd have to do the same for everyone."

No, retirement certainly did not happen naturally. I often think that the verb "to retire" should be expressed in the passive voice, "to be retired," and that disengagement should rather be called exclusion. For that is what happens. When we consider the important question of who benefits from this or that change, it is clear that it was not retired people whose needs were primarily being considered. Rather, they were being "pensioned off", since the emergence of the pension system was inseparable from the institutionalization of retirement.

The New Politics of Retirement

Retirement and the pension system evolved according to industrial and, later, political needs. At the same time they were crucial in the redefinition of the social obligations and relationships between workers and employers. This happened at a particular point in history, at a time when corporate and government bureaucracies were growing more centralized and increasingly dominating the life of society and its members.

Retirement did not really take hold until the years after World War Two, when the disengagement theorists attempted to portray it as part of the natural order of things. But the 1930s were an important decade in its acceptance by most Canadians. The high levels of unemployment – especially among young people – that accompanied the Depression were worrisome to politicians. Social unrest simmered and frequently reached the boiling point as people with neither work nor the prospects of work asked serious questions about the ability of the economy and society at large to meet their needs. One way of providing young people with jobs was to have old people retire.

This was the era of Franklin Roosevelt's New Deal in the United States and social planning ideas across the border were influential in Canada. Various organizations in the United States urged Roosevelt to bring in a government pension system. One of these groups, the California-based Townsend Movement, sketched a detailed plan for pensions for people over sixty and operated under the slogan "Youth for Work / Age for Leisure". A spokesman for the movement summed up its goals in rather bald terms in a letter to Roosevelt's Committee on Economic Security:

> Big business is too stupid to see that the Townsend Plan will be a
> means of giving it a new lease on life – that capitalism can only
> be saved by retiring permanently ten million of our old people,

and at the same time giving these old people the means by which to once more restore purchasing power in the United States.[4]

Although Roosevelt did not adopt the Townsend Plan, his government introduced a form of universal social security in 1935. This was one of the momentous achievements of his long presidency and provided an important foundation for his reputation as a great humanitarian. Old age assistance did not become available to the Canadian public at large until the Old Age Security Act was passed in 1951, in spite of the fact that Canada had introduced an Annuities Act as early as 1908 as a means of promoting thrift in the population. By 1936 all provinces had programs under the federal Old Age Pensions Act of 1927, but this was more a measure of poor relief since a very strict means test was applied and the amount of the pensions was insufficient to support recipients.

In 1979 the Canadian Senate Committee chaired by David Croll examined the issue of mandatory retirement at a time when the concept – not even a generation old – was coming under fire from all quarters. The Senate report, "Retirement Without Tears", summarized the implications of the U.S. move towards social security, noting that while farmers had worked until their bodies forced them to stop, by the time the Depression arrived the poorhouse awaited most workers. The report stated:

> Partly as a result of social security legislation in the United States in the mid-1930s, it came to be accepted in Canada that people should retire at 65 or close to 65. There was, of course, no law forcing people to retire at 65 but it became customary in many companies and government bodies. Sometimes compulsory retirement at 65 was built into the pension plan and became automatic.[5]

The Complexities of Compulsory Retirement

Things have changed in recent years. It has become obvious that mandatory retirement "isn't working" – figuratively as well as literally. The word "ageism" has crept into discussions of retirement as many of us have pointed out that compulsory exclusion from the workforce is discriminatory. At a time when women and people of colour struggle against sexism and racism, more old people have rejected the idea that they have to retire at sixty-five if they don't want to. It is an infringement of our basic human rights.

This position has been increasingly accepted over the past ten or fifteen years, to the extent that the Senate Committee on Retirement included in its 1979 report a principal recommendation that mandatory retirement be progressively abolished. "I think it's a terrible mistake", said Senator David Croll, "to throw people in the ash can".[6] Croll's views are reflected in the report, which advocates a much more flexible approach to retirement in both the public and private sectors.

This approach would recognize the variability of people's needs and desires when they get old. Some people who work at dirty, dangerous, or boring jobs often want to retire well before sixty-five – if they can afford to. Some people have just had enough of a particular job and want a change. Some people become sick and unable to work well before they reach the magic age.

But many others, especially in the group now called the "young-old" under the age of eighty, remain healthy and alert and have no desire to be shunted aside. Because the pension system is so pitifully inadequate, mandatory retirement frequently forces people into poverty by robbing them of the ability to sell the only asset they have – their labour power. But not only does mandatory retirement rob people of a decent income. More importantly, in our capitalist economy, status, too, flies out the window. In our society any group that doesn't have a job, whether youth, unemployed, or old, is disenfranchised, without power.

In the United States, mandatory retirement already seems to be on the way out. In 1979 the U.S. government did away with it in the public sector while raising the retirement age to seventy in the private sector. In Canada the winds of change seem to be blowing in the same direction.

Why the sudden change? Part of the answer lies in the increased agitation over the unfairness of the mandatory retirement system and the recognition that old people as a group are an embarrassing anomaly in a supposedly egalitarian society. Our situation is so bleak that Senator Croll's 1979 Report contained this rather startling recommendation: "The retired elderly should organize, protest and show militancy in order to improve their chances of achieving dignity, obtaining higher incomes, as well as medical and other services and finding useful work."[7] When was the last time you heard a government report urging the population on to militant political action?

Yet this recognition that so many of us who are in our later years are in dire straits does not fully explain why mandatory retirement has suddenly come under critical scrutiny. For one thing, compulsory retirement has other costs, relating to changes in the economy, in technology, and in the way work is performed. We hear a lot about high technology as the solution to our economic woes. Two people I know have a different point of view.

Alice and Esther both worked for the same insurance company for over ten years, ever since their children left home. Before that they did a lot of temporary and part-time office work to help their families get by. Alice's husband died, and the pension from his job at the warehouse of a large supermarket chain had no survivor's benefits. Esther had been separated for many years and was the sole support for her children.

As both women approached the age of sixty-five they wanted to stay on the job because, as women, their pensions would be small. They wanted to be able to live decently. In recent years Alice and Esther had taken the odd company retraining course to learn word processing, computerized filing, and the other new requirements of a job in a modern office. Under a new flexible retirement policy, their employer set up a performance appraisal committee of personnel specialists to help decide who could keep working and who had to retire. Some unionized companies have been forced to grant worker representation on such committees, but there are few unions representing clerical workers at insurance companies. Management claimed its system was fair and unbiased since the people who judge productivity were in the head office in another city and could apply objective standards.

So the committee carefully scrutinized Alice's and Esther's work and decided that Alice could not quite cut the mustard any more. Out she went, pensioned off. Her pension from the company was not indexed to increases in the cost of living, so it would soon be savaged by inflation. Esther was allowed to stay on in front of her video display terminal, but she often wondered when it would be her turn to be evaluated once again.

The American Management Association has realized that "Age is a poor predictor of both worker characteristics and worker performance".[8] Indeed, a flexible approach to retirement allows a company to save money. It can keep on its older employees who are still efficient rather than forcing them out and then paying for the training of younger workers.

So under current conditions and without disrupting the way things are organized in society, a new approach to retirement would be entirely possible. "Insurance companies will go for a later retirement age," observed one insightful businessman, "because if workers pay into the pension funds, the insurance companies will have larger funds to manage, on which they can make larger profits. Most big companies will probably agree to keep people on, provided that management has the right to terminate employment if a worker is inefficient or sick. Firing may present a problem. There may have to be some sort of job evaluation committee that will listen to the evidence and decide if a worker is being unjustly fired."[9]

This sort of hardheaded approach to the realities of retirement comes much closer to the mark than the theories of disengagement set out by some managerial personnel whose thinking is completely cut off from reality. The whole issue of retirement is a perfect example of this. The still-dominant ethic has it that retirement is an entirely natural transition, what the anthropologists call a rite of passage. But today, with so much unemployment among young people, there is more attention being paid to the negative psychological effects of excluding so many people from the workforce, especially since a job is such an important source of identity. If we find a way of guaranteeing income and status without work, surely, retirement ceases to be an issue.

The youth unemployment crisis is said to contribute to cynicism, despair, depression, and even suicide. In the same way, it is not hard to see why many old people faced with forced "disengagement" find it difficult to achieve what some have called "a successful retirement". Many can't imagine affording to live decently. Others, even those with adequate incomes, feel useless and lack a sense of purpose for living.

That is why I find it so distressing to hear otherwise intelligent people put forth theories about aging that ignore the existence of the unequal distribution of wealth and power in society. At best all the talk and theories are misguided. At worst they are attempting to justify continued inequality and hardship.

Given the present structures of society, retirement will always be a loaded word. For a relative few it means fulfillment: time to spend travelling or studying or engaged in some other long-postponed pursuit. More often – and especially for the majority of old people who live in or close to a poverty situation – it means difficult, messy decisions. Like Jessica they might have to consider a change of location, to a more "affordable" or practical place, a place they don't really want to be. It might mean a slow and painful separation from community, friends, or family. Often it means days alone spent watching TV, with occasional minor – but very real – blessings: an evening here or there with family, an afternoon here or there at a "sunshine club". At its worst, rather than fulfillment, retirement can only be described as disaster.

My husband George and I and our three daughters
at the Peace Garden in Boissevain, Manitoba in
1950.

5

The Emotional Maze –
Health and the
Business of Aging

Society has a moral obligation to insure that everyone has
access to an adequate level of health care to the end of life.
Compassion is the only valid bottom line.

TISH SOMMERS, *Gray Panthers Network*

I CANNOT THINK back on the last years of my father and
mother-in-law without a mixture of sorrow and anguish. Their
spouses had died relatively young, without experiencing the
nursing home or the hospital, though neither had enjoyed good
health. But for Father and Nana (as she was known to her family) there was no swift departure from this vale of tears – only
more tears, no matter how concealed or openly shed.

For these independent, family-loving people who had contributed so much in their lives, when ill health struck them in
their early eighties there was only the trauma of trying to make
a new life in a strange environment among strangers in hospitals and nursing homes. And yet in the 1960s it was the only
course that we, their families, could see. We were at a loss to

know what else to do.

When she knew that she couldn't continue to live in her own house any more, my mother-in-law had moved to her own apartment, close to me and another daughter-in-law. Although we each had full-time work we were able to pop in every day, do some shopping, and spend a few minutes chatting. Then early one morning I got a call from a neighbour who had found Nana lying on the floor of her apartment.

Although we tried to look after her at home, it soon became clear that Nana would have to go to the hospital, no matter how much she opposed this move. It had been her expectation that I would *never* let her be taken to hospital, much less to a nursing home. I had often tried to help her to know that there would be limits to what I could do, but the idea had remained. And now, in the face of the kind of care she would need, that limit had been reached. In the hospital she was disoriented, uncommunicative, and sometimes bordered on being abusive.

It became obvious that she would never again be able to live alone in her own place. After consulting her daughter in Saskatchewan, who was a farm wife raising three small children, we decided to put this sick, confused old woman in a nursing home.

By this time my work had made me familiar with a range of possibilities and I was under the impression that we had found her a spot in a good institution. That showed me how much I had to learn. Little did I know that the place was strictly regimented, with an orderly routine and rigid rules. This was just the wrong place for a woman who, from age three when her mother died, had made her own rules and regulations. She couldn't conform. So another place with less rigid rules was found. In so far as possible, the staff there treated the people as human beings, although human beings in a state of confusion and disorientation.

Even there, however, I would get phone calls from the staff, often late at night. Several times they called to ask me to come because she was sitting with her hat on waiting for someone to take her home. Each time I would head over in a state of fear. As I drove to the nursing home I would be thinking, "Will I be able to help her realize she must stay?" I would have liked to bring her home so that she could know some peace – but such a move was impossible. Even if I had not been working full-time (and there was no way I could do otherwise) I would not have been able to look after her properly. She needed help just to move and I couldn't lift her, she was a very heavy woman. I had no money, nor did she, to pay nursing care people even if they could be found.

Anyone who has been through this kind of experience knows the anguish of it all – the effort to steel oneself against the weakness of the moment when your loved one says, "How could you let this happen?" You think, maybe I could manage if only I tried harder. But you know it is out of the question from every angle – thought through in the hours when you should have been sleeping to get ready for the next day's problems – over and over again.

Then came another early-morning phone call, this time from my sister-in-law, who said that Nana had died in her sleep the night before. Our common thought was, "What a mercy!" But why are such "mercies" necessary?

Not too many years later, arthritis crippled my father so much that keeping up his own place became impossible. He stayed with each of his children but found that the change of routine, climate, and food was hard to adjust to, and with all the families so busy there was little time for the conversations he so cherished. His active mind could not bear to be without stimulus and he became frustrated with the inability of his body, wracked with arthritis, to cope. Soon enough he became a resident in a "home for the aged" in Brandon, Manitoba.

Sharing a small room with a stranger was difficult. It was a long time before father made friends with his neighbours. The ramps, the walker, and the attention of the staff made physical living less difficult for him. Although we tried hard, our visits were not all that frequent and letters could never take the place of family being there. Father understood the problems we had, but this understanding could not altogether make up for the loneliness he must have felt in this new situation.

Eventually a serious kidney infection put him in hospital.

After a long stay in the chronic care section, it was arranged that he would be taken to a nursing home. This was the final change he would have to endure, for my father lived out his last years there. At least he was back in Killarney, where family and old friends could drop by. Even this was possible only because the doctor, a friend of the family, said he would be responsible for care of my father's catheter. At that time nursing home legislation did not allow catheter patients to be accepted. An exception had been arranged, a rule bent.

Each time we had to make a decision about my mother-in-law or father there seemed to be little choice. But I will never forget the questions – both spoken and unspoken – of my loved ones about their fate. Recent studies show clearly that my anguished concern is shared by myriad other middle-aged children facing similar feelings of doubt and inadequacy. For me, the institutional arrangements we had to make for Nana and Father heightened my awareness of the aging process and its implications for all of us. This impressed me with the urgency of the need to think more deeply about old people in Canadian society.

Aging as Big Business

In April 1966 I left my job with the church in Winnipeg and moved to Toronto to work in the national office of the United Church as special assistant, senior adult work, with the Board of Christian Education. I was to be involved in leadership training for those who worked with older people, in production of a newsletter, and in developing programs for the church's homes for the aged.

From that time on into the early 1970s my job entailed a certain amount of travelling. The trips often gave rise to casual conversations with seatmates and other travellers and the conversation usually turned to my work on aging. I found out that most people were interested in the topic, sometimes because they were worried about their older family members, often because they simply wondered what would happen to them after they passed the magic age of sixty-five. Occasionally, too,

I met someone who had a more active interest in the field of aging. "Aging is big business, you know. We're building so many homes and care facilities. We can offer so much help in the selection of furniture, drugs, food services, janitorial equipment."

Salesmen leafed through their thick catalogues, pulling out glossy brochures advertising the latest products, asking for an opinion of their wares. In those early days of my work, even though I heard what was being said, it was all in passing. I didn't realize the implications of these fitful conversations about buildings, catering, pharmaceuticals, and the other aspects of planning for the elderly. I was involved in coming up with educational programs and materials beamed towards enhancing quality of life in the later years. I was too inexperienced with the area of institutional living to see how all the new products and services might have a dire influence on that quality of life. The structure of our Canadian society, as we became increasingly caught up in an urban life-style, was even then making old people a "problem" – lumped into the category of senior citizens – more recently, "seniors" – a group that needs care. Care itself was becoming a commodity to be merchandised.

Even loneliness, it would seem, is marketable. One drug company, Abbott Laboratories, portrays a despairing old man named George looking glumly into his teacup, the inevitable piece of toast untouched on the plate. "Alice isn't there any more," but "Ensure* is there to help". While we are assured that Ensure won't quite replace Alice's companionship or her good cooking, we are comforted that the product can alleviate "the nutritional risks of old age".[1]

I have come to realize that the condition and plight of the elderly have been manufactured just as surely as drugs like Hydergine and Ensure. This is where negative consumerism comes into play. Does anyone really want to consume the services of a hospital, nursing home, or psychiatric ward if the need for such consumption could be prevented?

Unfortunately, such consumerism is promoted by the aging industry, which revels in the new opportunities brought on by demographic changes. Headlines in the business sections of newspapers proclaim, "Investors See Opportunities in Health Care" and "Investment Opportunities Abound in Nursing Homes".[2]

At present, as the number of old people in Canada increases, so does the volume of business done by nursing home operators. The provision of care has become a very profitable business, with companies such as Extendicare making great strides every year. Extendicare has merged the many facets of its huge operation into a conglomerate called Crownx, in the health care section claiming to provide excellent care.

"Crownx posts profit rise of $12,520,000 in year".[3] It was plain to see where at least some of the company's profit had been spent: This newspaper item was followed a month later by a full-page advertisement, "Crownx Incorporated: New Mover in the World of Finance. And Health. And Technology." The Crownx Extendicare Group is now one of the largest providers of nursing-centre care and health-related services in North America.[4]

From the very beginning of my work in the field of aging I have seen far too many facilities run by administrators whose only preparation for their work was a course based on the methods of hospital administration or experience in financial management. And I'm left still to wonder whether most benefits don't accrue to economic analysts, computer software manufacturers, and shareholders rather than to the people living in their institutions or using their home care facilities.

If we look back over thirty years of activity in the area of homes for the aged, we can get an idea of how this peculiar process works. Providing homes for old people has become an industry, complete with personnel specialists, management consultants, experts in building design and finance, and administrative wizards. A government administrative apparatus has grown up alongside the industry to regulate the business. The whole thing has developed an amazing momentum of its own.

The cost of living in many homes is so high that only the wealthy can afford to live in them. Though there are subsidized places, these carry an inevitable stigma with them. People do not wish to be objects of charity. Many an old person has watched a beautiful-looking home being built in the neighbourhood and, upon applying to get in, has found that the costs make it impossible to live there, in spite of the exciting pre-building publicity that is inevitably generated.

As we reach middle age, we feel that gnawing sense of unease about the fate of our aging parents. We don't know what will happen to them, how they will manage. At the same time that we hear about the golden years, Golden Age clubs, and happy retirement villas, we are also deluged with reports of old people living in squalid, poorly ventilated rooming houses, subsisting on diets of tea and toast, without adequate security or fire protection.

So people look for their own particular solutions. In 1959, when I began my own work with old people, I saw many different attempts to deal with this problematic situation. Sometimes young and old family members lived together in the family home. Sometimes a parent or parents lived in the home or apartment of a single child, most often a daughter. Many of these young people held very demanding jobs. Often the possibility of marriage was put aside. Even so, I heard very little complaint about their lot. Jobs given up were nearly impossible to regain when the "care of aging parents" was ended – not to mention the jeopardy to their own future retirement income through the loss of pension benefits. Not all, but most, parents were appreciative even though they expected the sacrifice being made by their children.

But too often the death of the parents had a disastrous effect on the child. Suddenly, or more often after a long and arduous illness, the tremendous pressure was off and the son or daughter was alone. Since doors had been closed along the way, many were unable to build a life of their own or to contain the anger that had built up for so long.

The experience of such people made me realize how much work needed to be done in the area of family responsibility in an urban setting. I grappled with the question of how old people could maintain their independence in a society that now endorsed mandatory retirement at age sixty-five, which provided insufficient income, especially for women, to live out their years. There was little preparation for retirement. This was badly needed in a world which valued productivity above all else. How could old people cope with a drastic cut in income and a sudden shift to no longer having any apparent purpose? Little wonder that many felt useless, unwanted, of no value; and that the mortality rate for men, in those early days of mandatory retirement, went up noticeably between ages sixty-five and seventy.[5]

Rachel's Story

In February 1972 I went from my job with the United Church national office immediately into a position in a new home for the aged being built in downtown Toronto. I went into the job expecting to be the activities director, to set up both a program for the home and a centre for older people who lived in the neighbourhood. The centre was supposed to be built as soon as construction of the home was finished – but never was.

I was taking on a job that did not really fit my qualifications, but I thought it would be a good chance to put into practice some of the things I had learned about aging over the years. Once I started the job I found myself interviewing applicants who wanted to live in this beautiful new place. There was no official admissions policy but I quickly realized that if you had money and good health there was no problem. If you had only good health, it was another matter. Living in the home would cost more than many of the people I interviewed could afford.

I later learned that disappointment and disillusion were only delayed for many who did take up residence. If they became sick, their money would not help secure them their own spot and they were told they would have to leave, in poor health and that much older. The problem is, governments restrict their reimbursements for nursing care to a certain limited number of hours. In Ontario the law provides for only one and a half hours of daily nursing care for each resident.[6] For those who either appear to need or actually do need more than the allotted hours, few options exist.

A friend of mine, Rachel, decided after a few years of retirement to stop living in her own place. At one time Rachel had been a successful businesswoman. Now, with no close family, she was an independent, self-reliant person whose income meant that she could afford a beautiful single room in the new home for the aged where I was working.

As admissions officer it was my job to interview Rachel about coming into the home. This was one of the easier interviews. Rachel knew exactly what she wanted. We had it, she could pay for it, and there were no obstacles.

The change worked out well for Rachel. The location was excellent, the room exactly what she had envisioned, the meals just to her taste. Rachel was friendly and soon she and the others on her floor were into bridge, tea parties, or shopping trips. She started to develop relationships that were closer to family than any she had known in her adult life. She looked much younger than her years seemed to indicate. She was active on several committees – library, residents' council, finance. For many years her room was a home where she could entertain friends, read, and watch the TV news. She expected to be there for the rest of her life. She seemed to feel that the personnel in her new surroundings could be counted on as a substitute family.

Although I left my job at the home after only one year, I kept in touch with Rachel and her friends for the next ten years. Then, ill health struck Rachel. First came cataracts and glaucoma, followed by an operation that resulted in near total loss of sight. The trauma began to have an effect on her general state of health. Eventually she had a fall brought on by a combination of poor vision and someone moving her chair to an unfamiliar spot in the room. The administration of the home decided she could no longer manage alone.

It was convenient for the staff to have Rachel close to the nursing station, so she was moved to a double room, in which the other woman smoked. Although her personal privacy was one of her most prized possessions, it seemed to be of no concern to the decision-makers. This bright, self-reliant woman started to speak with longing about death. It held no fear for her. What *was* terrifying was what would happen in the rest of her life, since the home was not set up to provide the kind of care she now needed.

The days passed and Rachel was in a constant quandary about what to do, until one day she had a sudden heart failure. She was sent – unaccompanied – by ambulance to the hospital. When I phoned the place she'd called home for so many years to ask about her, no one could tell me anything. Although Rachel had made many friends among the residents, there was no close feeling for Rachel among the staff who were in control.

She received excellent care in the hospital and I found that the people in charge were very understanding. Although it had seemed unlikely, Rachel did recover sufficiently to leave the hospital to live in a nursing home, in an unfamiliar part of the city. She was happy with the care she received there, and arranged for the installation of a phone. Things seemed to be going well, but soon there was another fall and another hospital. This was followed by a return to the nursing home, and then another stint in a second hospital where friends found her totally unaware of who she was, who they were, and where she was.

Our anger and frustration reached a high pitch, and now we really tried to make arrangements for someone to be with her – perhaps a nursing assistant, or just a companion – so that there might be some thread of continuity for her as she lived the uncertain life of being shunted back and forth from hospital to nursing home. I undertook the task of finding out from the trust company that handled her affairs how we could arrange this. I knew she could afford such care, and we all felt she should have it, but I wasn't sure whether the funds would be available.

I should have known the trust company official would say, "It's not that easy." It would take them time to assess the situation, but they would look into it. Now it was out of our hands – and Rachel's. The trust company, a doctor, and the nursing home together would decide what was best for Rachel and if *they* felt there was a need for a companion or a nurse, the trust company would arrange it. Since Rachel had no family or proxy, the trust company was in charge of all the funds. It had the power, for Rachel was said to be too ill by then, and too confused, to make decisions by herself. The nursing home would have to agree to have the extra person around. The trust company would need a doctor's order to proceed. This took a lot of time to work out, given the complexities of the law and the busy schedules of those involved.

Rachel's friends, who knew very well that this could happen, should have been more aggressive much earlier. In retrospect, it's so clear. The friends who tried to be Rachel's real family – people who were well aware of the problems of nursing homes – were unable to get around these complexities in time to help Rachel. So much for our belated, albeit well-meaning, efforts on her behalf. We really didn't have much to say in the matter, for when it came right down to it, it really did not matter what happened to yet another old woman who was alone – lost in a sea of referrals. But miracles can happen. Rachel finally received institutional permission to have someone with her for part of each day. A few days after the companion started coming, Rachel died. The effort we had made was too little and much too late.

There are many Rachels in Canada, and in other parts of our world, too, it seems. In Japan, for instance. Jean Oda May, in the introduction to Yasushi Inoue's book on the aged in Japan, writes:

> Many of Japan's aged are now less fortunate than the author's mother, whose family adhered to the Confucian ideal of honouring and cherishing the old. In Japan, as in the West, the elderly today are frequently shunted aside, ignored, or made to feel they are a burden. A sad commentary of this state of affairs is that at special temples for the aged in Japan, the penitents increasingly pray for an early death.[7]

The Rachels of our world do not even have a special temple to go to, but I know there are old people all around us, tucked away in nursing homes or other institutions or even in a spot of their own, who join the Rachels in making their desperate prayers for death every day.

It is maddening that Rachel's "story" occurs on an everyday basis all over the country. It is a very important part of the environment out of which the nursing home industry has sprung. And sprung it has, almost to the top of the country's most profitable corporations.

Since I know very well what troubles for residents can arise in a "non-profit" situation, I am horrified to contemplate how these could be multiplied in an institution run for profit. Although not impossible, it seems to me very improbable that the urge for profit could benefit anyone but the owner – whether an individual or a large corporation. So I believe that we, old and young alike, must be much more aware and alert to the meaning behind the headlines about the booming health-care business.

Such undertakings have been and are now going ahead very rapidly and with government blessing. In Ontario one study, "Caring for Profit: The Commercialization of Human Services in Ontario", showed that 90 per cent of Ontario's 333 nursing homes in 1983 were operated for profit.[8] The same report warned of the potential for serious and far-reaching consequences for this province and the rest of Canada if the trend to reliance on profit-based health care and social services increases without careful investigation into such enterprises. As a result, the Social Planning Council asked the Ontario government to place a "moratorium on commercialism of human services" until an appropriate review had been undertaken.[9]

Meanwhile, we have arrived at a point where governments are looking for ways to cut expenditures on social programs and business is eyeing the opportunity to make money, while appearing to help the aged. It is a dangerous point, and it may be too late to add our voices to those who have been trying to help us to see that institutional living is not for everyone and is, in fact, only welcomed by or necessary for a very small number, and that there must be alternatives.

Sickness and Health in Old Age

Although some of us have always known that the causes of sickness among old people are not necessarily those that require medical diagnosis, it is only recently that there has been a broader concern with the preventive measures that can minimize the consumption of expensive hospital services. The preventive measures must include sufficient income, affordable housing, and community services like multi-service centres, day hospitals, and day care for old people.

We need more meals on wheels and transportation geared to our needs. We need more programs like the one we set up in the 1960s, the Sunshine Club in Winnipeg. This experience made me realize the value of a multi-service centre in a community where so many older people were having serious problems adjusting to the loss of a spouse, a move, or less robust health.

A relatively few old people do develop chronic disease or disabilities and require a special brand of care. But it must truly be "care" and it must not be an uncaring service that "dumps" them in a corner of a shabby room in a commercially-run nursing home, with insufficient attention to their needs and leaving them only to wait for death. These nursing homes, as writer Daniel Jay Baum says in his book *Warehouses for Death*, are all too often places where the aged "may survive in body, but this does not mean that they survive in mind and spirit".[10]

An example of the better kind of care is the Bernard Betel Centre for Creative Living on the northern edge of Toronto – a program not unlike the Sunshine Club, but much larger. Space at the centre has been carefully planned to accommodate as many activities as needed. There are expandable meeting rooms, a chapel, health centre, woodworking space and equipment, craft space with supplies, music rooms, cafeteria, and lounge.

Here is a positive alternative to isolating the old in residential institutions. The idea at the Bernard Betel Centre is that older people participate in thinking about, planning for, and carrying out the programs they need and want. The space is their space. The people who come to the centre are in charge – although, clearly, they are assured of continuing support from the sponsors if and when problems arise that for some reason or other they can't manage to solve themselves.

This kind of facility with its various programs enables many people – old and young – who now occupy acute-care beds to remain in their own homes where they really want to be, while at the same time freeing up space for those people who really need hospitalization.

My contacts with and increasing knowledge of old people whose health and / or money runs out have made me wonder what's ahead for the many old people who live past the age of eighty-five. Certainly, my own views on living arrangements as I get older have changed markedly from an earlier time when I had simply assumed that when I retired I would live in one of those "nice" senior citizens' apartments I had read about and even visited in my work. I don't have much use for the tag "senior citizen" but at the time I had managed to put aside my aversion. Becoming more aware of the facts about such housing, as well as the nature of my retirement, made me realize how mistaken I had been to "simply assume" I could move into such a building.

Although I'm now retired, I've continued, and hopefully may continue, to live in a small apartment close to the important things in my life – my family and friends. Being near to shopping, transportation, a post office, or banking, are especially important for an old person, and I have this as well. For a single woman with my income, affordable housing is almost nonexistent in Toronto so I do pay more for rent than the budget planners say I can afford; as do countless others in my income bracket. But I can have my family and friends come visit when I want to. Most important of all, I am in control of my own life and I intend to keep it that way as long as it is within my power to do so.

My word for good health is well-being, something that has been high on my list of priorities for a long time. But for a person of my age, the possibility that a change in health will shake up my world is always there. Your state of health has a tremendous bearing on where you can live. And where you live has an enormous effect on the state of your well-being, as I learned in a recent bout of illness that lasted several months.

Combined with what I see happening to many of my older friends, it made me realize just how basic our health is to remaining in control of our lives. Because I felt so sick and was coughing a lot, I didn't go out or see anyone except for a few family members. I tried to put on a good front for them but inside I was really beginning to believe the things I'd heard about how "health would inevitably deteriorate after the age of seventy". I had previously pooh-poohed this notion but now I started to think that I would never get well again – a depressing frame of mind, to say the least.

Gradually, though, the virus seemed to clear and I began to sleep at night instead of lying awake coughing. Then out of the blue came another bug. Flu this time, with a high fever. I knew I needed the help of my doctor, and he prescribed an antibiotic. Almost at once my situation improved and soon I was well enough to attend the annual meeting of the Canadian Association on Gerontology in Moncton. It was a good move. Seeing friends, being involved with the sessions, and being stimulated by new information got me going again and I slowly regained a sense of my own well-being. I put behind me the creeping fears that so nearly overtook me when I was ill.

Thinking about that terrible time, I realize how fortunate I was to be in my own place and to have had knowledge of the process of aging so that I could examine what I was experiencing. Without my knowledge and work on aging I might have given up. It has become very clear that the physical illness itself is not the main danger, but rather the temptation to give up trying to be well – to accept the myth that to be old is to be sick, a myth I'd always resisted with vigour.

Two other pieces of luck were with me. My doctor was not one of the many who tell old people, "It's just your age." He did not prescribe drugs unless it was absolutely necessary. Also, my family needed me, even though I couldn't help them nearly as much as I wanted to. For many people my age, none of these positive circumstances prevail when illness hits.

Even in the best of situations, managing illness and the possibility of non-recovery and death requires great strength of mind, and courage. For instance, my friend Barbara, who lived close by my apartment, was active, fiercely independent, and enrolled in several university courses. One day her usual jaunty and cheerful manner seemed strangely subdued. I had heard that she was facing a recurrence of a serious illness. She mentioned that her health wasn't too good and that she was seeing a doctor regularly. But it was not fear of illness or even death that was gnawing at her spirit. Rather, she too was worried about what would become of her if her health became permanently impaired but she *did not* die.

"That's the most worrying thing," she said with a shake of her head. "I don't want to be dependent and I don't know what I can do to avoid it." But she did find a way. With help from her doctor and support from her son and a group of close friends, she managed in her own apartment until she knew it was impossible to go on. Then she gave up her place and went into hospital, where she died within a few weeks. To me, it was a case of courage in the extreme – and it is more commonly found than you might think.

One man I worked with dealt in a very positive way with the pitfalls of nursing home experience. Wilfred Scott was a bachelor, an ardent churchman, and professional psychologist who was deeply concerned with all aspects of the aging process. For many years he had done education for aging, actively working for better employment conditions for older workers, and promoting more stimulating experiences to keep the minds of old people alive. All of this was accomplished against a background of uncertain physical health as he lived with the aftermath of an early stroke and the discipline required to control Parkinson's disease.

For a time he did quite well in an apartment building that provided housekeeping and meal service. But the Parkinson's eventually got out of control and he had to be hospitalized. While he was still in hospital a social worker managed to find a place in a nursing home. His relatives approved, and Wilfred Scott went from the hospital to a nursing home.

This was a big mistake. The staff at the new place made no attempt to get to know him. Evidently they seldom thought about providing stimulating activities for the residents. Perhaps they did not have time for this. They were too few in number to work at any length with any one person, and too poorly paid to think of anything but how much their feet hurt. They had trouble controlling their impatience with the people who needed their attention. There were even occasional staff members who hated the whole scene so much they became needlessly rough and unfeeling. Staff would turn the television off and on according to their own whims. They would frequently ignore or put off responding to requests for help. The staff spoke about the residents as if they were children and often addressed them to their faces as if they were toddlers.

But worst of all was the total disregard for each person's need for and right to privacy. Even though many of the residents needed personal care because they were sick, the home made no effort to ensure individual attention and treat the residents as if they were people who had unique wants and needs.

One day Wilfred Scott was feeling tired and asked one of the staff if she would help him out of his chair and back to his room. Rushing by, she paused to pat him on the head. "There, there, dearie," she smiled. "You aren't really tired." After enduring as much patronizing indignity and humiliation as he could stand, he managed to stop a visitor who helped him to his feet. He went to his room, picked up the telephone, and found himself a new place to live in Central Park Lodge, part of a large chain of posh retirement homes. He got his belongings together and signed himself out.

As a single person who could afford costly accommodation, Dr. Scott was in a position to take this kind of action and it was a happy solution for him. His one fear was that such expensive accommodation would eat up the money he wanted to be used for establishing a scholarship for undergraduates in gerontology. His fear proved to be groundless. The Wilfred G. Scott Fellowship is very real and has been used already by several students.

In this regard, I can't help thinking of some friends of mine, a couple in their eighties, people reasonably independent and well off. They were used to living in a large apartment that gave them lots of working space. Paula was a writer and David an artist. They had both worked for the government for many years and had held positions of responsibility. Paula, always a tough and wiry woman, began to develop a condition that affected her balance, but with the help they could afford to hire and the support of her companion she and David managed to look after themselves, and enjoy life.

Eventually Paula needed nursing care, and David found that his eyesight was failing to a point that he could no longer provide the support her worsening condition demanded. They faced the difficulty of finding living accommodation for a couple in a facility that could give them the care they needed. This proved to be a big headache for themselves, their family, and the friends who tried to help. Nursing homes where a couple can continue to live together are few and far between.

After a time, a place was found. The room had the usual bed, chair, and dresser and enough room for a piece of their own furniture with its life-long associations. A chair for Paula now meant a wheelchair, so their room was even more crowded. But they managed to maintain some of their usual gracious hospitality. They offered me sherry in their own lovely glasses when I came to visit.

One evening when I phoned to ask if it would be all right to visit, they told me that there was some entertainment planned for the residents that night and invited me to join them. The whole occasion turned into a sorry mess and I had no opportunity to even talk with my friends, because the music was too loud and there were repeated, vigorous and inept attempts by the staff to get people to sing and dance. I came away sad and discouraged. The staff had honestly tried to provide a good time for the residents, but they had no concept of what the residents themselves saw as a good time. The problem starts with the firmly entrenched notion that staff must be "doing" for "these people" in "our" home – "poor old souls". And so the staff does not even consult the people who are supposed to benefit from their efforts.

A few months later Paula and David asked me to join them for a Christmas luncheon. It was obviously a very special occasion, with carefully decorated tables set out for groups of four, six, and eight people. The food was excellent and well presented. But once again the so-called entertainment spoiled the whole thing. There was loud music, a scantily-clad female singer and coy, ageist remarks from board members at the head table. To cap it all off, there was a raucous visit from Santa – frankly, most of us felt a little beyond that.

If only the people who had organized the event had thought about the people who were going to be there. We were looking forward to simply being with close friends and sharing a special Christmas luncheon, and perhaps exchanging news of other friends and old neighbourhoods from which we were now isolated. We all just wanted quiet conversation with a bit of dignity. The people who ran the home failed to consider us as human beings who might have specific ideas about what constituted a good time.

In the end, David excused himself early from our table because his hearing aid was just picking up the excessive din in the room, even though he had been careful to adjust it for conversation with his friends at the table. David and Paula said later that they felt depressed because their room was too small to allow a visit from all three of their invited guests. More than ever, they had the feeling that the world was moving its walls closer and closer around them, shutting out any real room to move, breathe, and be themselves.

It would be easy to improve human communication with old people by recognizing that we often have problems with hearing, vision, and speaking. What happened to Paula and David reflects the tendency to see old people as negative stereotypes who need and want to be entertained and amused in whatever way is fashionable at the time. Old people cease to be real people and become a distinct and inferior group who need to be taken care of because they can't cope for themselves. It became impossible to meet David and Paula's expectations – or mine, for that matter – because we weren't seen as having any in the first place.

A Matter of Considerable Choice

Remembering all these experiences provokes my anger, and especially when I hear politicians attempting in the name of fiscal restraint to make family members feel guilty about not supporting their aging parents. Those who don't support their parents are few; those who find it hard economically are many.

An issue of *Chatelaine*, for instance, discusses the various ways middle-aged people can find the best possible environment and proper care for their parents.[11] The article says that having old people stay put, move in with their children, or find a new place to live are the possible options, but that whichever way is chosen there will be problems. This is because there are many levels of care and many services. Some overlap and compete with one another. Things are largely unco-ordinated. As a newspaper article put it, "The major support appears to be their own families and some of the children's struggles seem heroic."[12]

If we could just get the "heroes" and the "useful" services together, many problems would fade away. In fact, we do seem to be heading in this direction. On all sides there is discontent with present arrangements for health care for the elderly. We're beginning to understand and take action on the importance of preventive measures towards improvement of the quality of life in the later years.

Right now, in Canada, some government planning bodies and many non-governmental groups are working with immense energy to bring about needed changes. One group, Concerned Friends of Ontario Citizens in Care Facilities, has been lobbying for reform in nursing home care. Some of us, who are old, are part of that effort, but more of us need to become informed about what's going on – not just for old people, but for everyone – and to become active in our support for the lives of all Canadians. Such measures would include adequate income for all, affordable housing, knowledge of how to keep well, day care for people who need it, of whatever age, and of course how best to share the resources we each have so that there would be a lessening of the sense of uselessness, boredom, loneliness, and lack of purpose in living which so many, old and young, now know.

So it is basically a matter of choice. We have to rearrange our priorities. When I was growing up there wasn't much money around and although our family got by, it was a "no-frills" life.

What we had was a sense of community, a knowledge that if we really needed help our friends and neighbours would be there. But today we live in a society in transition. The communities I knew as a child and in my years in the north no longer exist across the country. I noticed the change when I moved to Winnipeg in the 1950s and, later, to Toronto. I was part of the change in our society. It is represented in my life.

Today I live in a fragmented type of society where speed, efficiency, and growth take priority. As I look at the city around me I see not only the "poor, old folks". I also see lots of luxury condominiums being built. Shopping malls continue to spring up. Debate rages over an eleven-billion-dollar nuclear power plant down by the lakeshore, a plant being built to supply electricity no one seems to need.

It all reminds me of a passage from Senator Croll's 1966 report on aging. The report quoted Lewis Mumford, the famous American student of technology and urban design. During the 1950s Mumford was worried about the effects on old people of the North American trend towards sprawling suburbs, shopping centres, and automobiles. These new communities were designed with cars, not old people, in mind. You have to travel a mile or two by car just to buy a loaf of bread. These were communities which had no real place for old people.

Senator Croll must have seen this too, because his report included Mumford's startling assessment of industrial capitalism in the postwar years, when mandatory retirement was the norm and pension plans were expanding. According to Mumford, the first step towards framing a "sound program" for old people was to examine the human situation as a whole, not just focus on individual problems of destitution, disease, or hospital care. There could be no short cut to improved care for the aged.

To do well for the aged, Mumford said, "We must give a new direction to the life of the whole community." In fact, he suggested that such care and the all-important rebuilding of human communities would need to receive "something like the zeal, the energy, the skill, the dedication we give to the monomaniac production of motor cars and super-highways". And he warned, "If we fail here, we shall, in prolonging life, only prolong the possibilities of alienation, futility, and misery."[13]

Despite Mumford's very articulate warning – and some twenty years after the Senate report trumpeted it to the Canadian public – I am afraid that when I walk out onto the streets near my apartment I still see far more motor cars than old people. The cars rush past the corner where I wait to cross, bearing their noisy, polluting, and often dangerous witness to our fragmented society.

6

Development Education – and Action

What else should our lives be but a continual series of beginnings, of painful settings out into the unknown, pushing off from the edges of consciousness into the mystery of what we have not yet become, except in dreams.

DAVID MALOUF, *An Imaginary Life*

WHILE WORKING in the field of aging for nearly twenty-five years, in rural and urban settings, in church and community institutions, as a paraprofessional adult educator and innovator of programs for old people, I saw the great differences in how we age, in the vital living that can be, in the understanding possible between young and old. Over the years of my work and as I grow older I've had exceptional opportunities to observe and learn more about this inevitable process – aging. Still, I often have the sense that our efforts to address the issues of aging have been focused on its most easily discerned and more superficial aspects. As Rhea Shulman, director of the Bernard

Betel Centre for Creative Living, remarked sadly to me, "You know, no one is really *thinking* about aging."

In the late 1950s and early 1960s, when I worked in a local church, I was involved in leadership development at regional and provincial levels. Later my work was in the national office of the United Church, where my particular niche was the development of programs both with and for older adults. Throughout this time I thought I could see an effort by the church to become aware of how best, in a changing world, to minister to the well-being of all its people, young and old. News was in the air about the production of exciting new resource materials. Training centres had been set up in four regions across Canada to help develop new approaches to leadership. To these centres came every kind of group – families, church-school teachers, ministers, young people, old people, women's groups, men's clubs, community groups.

Those of us in leadership roles put a lot of time, thought, and effort into considering how best to work on new approaches and new educational programs. How could we share our excitement about new educational resources that helped us to discover for ourselves the meaning of the Christian faith? How does a Christian education relate to the issues of everyday life? What are the best means of encouraging better and more honest, open communication between people?

For many, the Sunday School class, the young people's group, the women's organization, the men's club – whatever particular group we were involved in – seemed the place to work on educational issues. The resources provided us with plenty of ideas and ways for a new kind of teaching and learning.

Many of us were deeply interested in seeing some of the church "walls" come down. Our concerns ranged from matters of formality – we thought, for instance, that there should be less rigidity of dress in pulpit and pew – to democratic principles. We argued that women should serve equally on church boards, that young and old should both share in management, and that children should be recognized as an integral and involved part of the congregation. In short, we believed that more attention should be paid to bringing the realities of personal and social life into the church. We felt that worship should mean discovering rather than accepting.

As it turned out, not all church members were excited about these possibilities, and in fact many people who were in the upper parts of the church hierarchy seemed to have felt threatened. As we heard warnings of budget cuts and of the need to rethink our responsibilities, it seemed to me that there was no way that the builders of the man-made structures and organization of the church would agree to this new way of working, in which their control and management of affairs might be lost. There seemed an intense pressure within the structures of the church to go back on the changes that many of us thought so important, to return to an emphasis on indoctrination rather than follow the route of social and self-discovery.

Frustrated by these battles and by what seemed to be a backward trend, I decided to have done with old structures, or so I thought. Being alone made it easier for me. I wanted to continue to live my life in the light of my belief in the possibility of significant change, in a new time when the race for power and material possessions, in which people are pawns to be used, would give way to the struggle for a society in which people have the highest value.

I resigned from my church position in the fall of 1971, to be effective in January 1972. Without either enough information or thought on my part, in February 1972 I took the job in the new home for the aged. I was to be activities director and would work with a centre for the surrounding community's older people. Nothing turned out as I had expected. I resigned from that job in January 1973, wiser but very sad.

Working in New Directions

Now I had unscheduled time – a situation I hadn't experienced for a long time. But once again a combination of family and friends led off in a completely unexpected – and rewarding – direction. My daughter Judith had been to work in the West

African country of Ghana in a Volta River resettlement program. Now back in Canada, she had continued her involvement in African issues by joining a newly formed organization called the Toronto Committee for the Liberation of the Portuguese African Colonies – known popularly by its acronym, TCLPAC (pronounced "tickle-pack"). TCLPAC was a support group for the struggles of the people in Angola, Guinea-Bissau, and Mozambique to gain their independence from Portugal's harsh colonial rule.

Among other activities TCLPAC members sponsored a film series to help educate themselves and other Canadians about what was going on in Southern Africa and other parts of the world. I became a regular participant at these film showings and through them I came to know another group of young people who worked out of the Development Education Centre (DEC), some of them members of TCLPAC as well.

DEC was a recently formed non-profit collective organization – that is, a group of workers who, theoretically, share equal responsibility for managing and conducting various programs, projects, and business matters. The centre distributed and sold books and films, ran a resource library, and produced a radio program. It was generally engaged not only in doing research and providing information on the countries of the Third World but also in exploring issues of underdevelopment in Canada.

I had encountered groups of young people throughout my work in the church, but this group seemed to be a different breed. Encouraged by their interest in my concerns around the issues of aging, I began to work with them, first as a volunteer and then as a member of the collective. Much to my surprise and delight, I experienced a profound change in the role I played. Before, in church organizations, I had often found myself designated as a leader; in fact I had been trained for that role. With DEC the structure of work became a kind of shared learning experience, somewhat like the way of working we had been discovering through the new curriculum the church had produced in the early 1960s. There was opportunity for leadership if your experience suited the situation.

As part of the DEC collective, a whole new vista unfolded. I got to know people who were trying to work towards the kinds

of changes in our society that I thought were needed. Until that
time I had not discovered a group willing and able to safeguard
the freedom to risk the hard work involved in such an
endeavour. I found myself in a rare and special kind of relationship. Here I was, a frustrated woman in her late sixties involved
with a group of people, the oldest of whom was over thirty
years younger than myself. They seemed to understand my disillusion with the kinds of structures I had recently left. They
challenged me to do something about my discouragement,
especially with what I saw happening in the field of aging.

As a result of this connection the years from 1974 to 1980,
when I was part of the DEC collective, were a time of new richness and growth in my life experience. I was able to discuss and
think about things that were going on around me, things I had
certainly perceived before but had not fully spelled out for
myself. Why the church programs had, in my mind, ultimately
failed. Why I was so hostile to the labelling of old people as
senior citizens. What labelling was all about. What I had really
meant the time I had complained in the church's *Senior Adult
Newsletter* that old people were categorized simply by the way
we talked about "we" and "they". Why I had been upset in my
brief administrative position in the home for the aged over the
kind of business bargaining that was so widespread. Contradictions became more clearly visible.

For instance, there was the fact that not all old people are
thought of as "senior citizens". The rich and the famous retain
their identity. Others simply refuse to be labelled, even though
it is easier in our system if one just accepts labels and whatever
advantages or disadvantages they bring. I became certain that
there were old people in Canada who were not willing to be
labelled and slotted into various convenient categories of service delivery, whether it was special housing or how to occupy
one's time. I realized I should try to find new ways of dealing
with the negative images of aging, and that I should work on
developing new initiatives around a more positive view of
aging.

In 1974 my co-workers at DEC helped me to write a position
paper that we sent to people across Canada who we thought
might be interested in issues of aging. The paper began with a

quote from the Saskatchewan Senior Citizens' Commission:
"The elderly for the most part are segregated from the mainstream of society. With the advent of retirement and thus the
loss of productive worth, the elderly are pushed to one side."[1]

Based on the assumptions I had made from my knowledge
and work in the field of aging, we stated that "aging is for everyone", that both youth and old age are part of the same life cycle.

> And so, from a time when most of the discussion of aging cen-
> tred on material needs, we turn now to broader questions about
> the society which is turning a natural process into a "problem."
> No one can or would wish to deny the need of older people for
> more money, more and better accommodation, lower fares for
> travelling, adequate recreational facilities and so on. However,
> older people also need and some want to engage in analysis of
> what is happening and what should be happening in the society
> of which we are a part. If people are to live, rather than merely
> exist, in their later years, they must have access to suitable
> resources which will enable them to prepare their own programs
> for analyzing the social, economic and political structures relat-
> ing to current issues in the world.

That mimeographed position paper was the start of my involvement in a project that would consume most of my time,
thought, and energies for the greater part of the next decade of
my life-span. During that period the DEC collective continued
to provide understanding and support, a source of ideas, and
most of all my valued reference point in the face of so much
that was happening.

The response to the position paper was encouraging, and DEC
people were accomplished fundraisers. We raised a small
amount of money and started up Development Education and
Action (DEA), "a program with Senior Adults".

DEA in Action

DEA started out as a small discussion group exploring the problems of aging in society. We would hold meetings during the
day in an accessible place, close to public transportation. They

were attended by men and women in the Toronto area who had responded to the position paper.

Most of the seven original members were former colleagues from the recently disbanded United Church Committee for Senior Adults. These people had a number of things in common: an interest and involvement in social issues; a wish to change the negative images of aging; and an enthusiasm for the opportunity to examine these issues and try to work out solutions. From that first handful of members DEA grew to a membership of over fifty, with countless contacts across the country.

The first time DEA got together we looked at a National Film Board documentary, "Nell and Fred", about housing for old people in Canada. Later we had meetings to discuss the anti-colonial struggles in Southern Africa, the problems of small farmers in Ontario, and Canada's aid program to the Third World. Members related their impressions of time spent in other countries – teaching, working as a doctor, and observing the conditions of old people. It became apparent to us that both Canada's aid to developing countries and our "doing for" people here in Canada netted the same result – a debilitating state of dependency for countries and people. We felt then that as old people we had to do something to change the situation for other old people, at least here in Canada. We wanted to put the principles of self-sufficiency and self-reliance into practice.

We decided to produce a slide-tape show on aging, for use as an educational resource. The federal government had just come up with a "New Horizons Program for Senior Citizens", so we made a proposal to that program for funds to finance our undertaking. What a fuss! If we had asked for the moon it would have been easier. There was money available for choirs, crafts, and feeding birds, but for education? For, by, and about old people? That was a different thing. Education and learning were for the young. Old people were through with that and needed help with leisure-time activities to fill in the days and years of retirement. So went the rhetoric. The initial response from the agency was just the kind of wrong-headedness we wanted to change.

Eventually, after continued discussion and our insistence on the importance of our proposal, the regional New Horizons program director recommended our project and we got a grant. Now, as I look back on these efforts of ours in 1975-76, I'm not sure that either we or the New Horizons person in our region recognized our struggle to be funded for what it was.

The whole purpose of DEA was to give voice, with the resources we had or could create, to the dismay we felt over the treatment of old people lumped together as "senior citizens". In our publicity for that first slide-tape montage we said that our study and discussion about growing old had shown us "the need to clarify in our own minds how we are understood and misunderstood by the power groups and image-makers of contemporary society". At a DEA meeting, one of our members said, "Old people don't have to be satisfied with what is now!" Neither do young people, we added. From the first our group was old and young working together.

We hoped our proposed slide-tape presentation would stimulate such thinking and discussion. We called it *These Old Ones: Growing Old in Canada and China Then and Now*, choosing China for a couple of reasons. One of our members had been a medical missionary in China for thirty years before coming back to Canada, where he set up a public health system in Ontario. I had also just visited China on a study tour with the Canadian Association for Adult Education and had observed the conditions and roles of old people there.

In the beginning the DEA members had very little knowledge of audio-visuals of any description, let alone of how to produce a slide-tape show. We felt we had a lot of things we wanted to say about issues of aging, but weren't sure of the techniques required to say them. But the DEC people encouraged us to go ahead, promising us help along the way if we needed it. We did need help, and they gave it generously, but did not take over our role as producers of our own resource.

After we finished *These Old Ones* in 1976, we used it extensively across the country. We would either send it out to a group or take it along and conduct workshops ourselves. The workshops varied in length and location. I participated in two sessions that were each a week long. One of these was in Montreal, where a friend arranged a week of showings for groups of old people and students of gerontology at McGill University. I spent one evening presenting the slide-tape show to a group of professionals who were friends of my hosts. The discussions were always lively and there never seemed to be enough time to finish them.

A community college in Terrace, B.C. arranged another week-long series of showings. We did some promotion through the local news media, and every morning I showed the slide-tape *These Old Ones* and talked with women from different parts of the community. On the last morning, all the groups met together. Several good suggestions came out of this meeting, especially about how old people and young people might be of benefit to one another if they only knew each other better. We also showed *These Old Ones* to the residents and staff of a home for the aged, with a second showing for staff who missed the first one because they were on duty.

We travelled up the Skeena River to Smithers for a community showing in a new home for senior citizens. After a quick interview by the local radio station I went over to the nearby town of Hazelton for a meeting with the local health care workers and a showing to a band council meeting of Native people. When I returned to Terrace I showed the montage to a group of community college teachers and participated at a weekend women's conference. I remember getting a little upset when one earnest and well-meaning young reporter in Terrace referred to me in his news story as "Doris Marshall, sixty-six years *young*" (my emphasis). He seemed to have missed the entire point: You don't have to be young to be an activist, to produce slide-tape shows, to engage people in discussion. In fact it helps – dare I say it is better in many ways? – to be old.

These Old Ones was getting around. We met with such a positive response that DEA decided to make another slide-tape show. This time the message we wanted to get across was that, for the most part, we old people wanted to remain in our own homes and that we needed helpful community services if this were to be possible. We had established enough credibility by this time that funding was no problem.

In our second slide-tape show, *In Our Own Homes*, DEA focused its attention on the lack of choices old people face due to insufficient income, the scanty supply of affordable housing, the inaccessibility of many community services, and the almost total lack of preventive health information. The montage *In Our Own Homes* was an attempt to help us see clearly that there must and can be choices other than a home for the aged or a nursing home. It seemed obvious to us that if all old people had a decent income to allow proper nourishment, suitable housing, access to useful community services, and the chance to make a meaningful contribution to society, then the loneliness and confusion that often lead people directly into institutions would be dramatically reduced. These factors would lessen the necessity for such a move. We hammered home the message that the elderly are not a problem; rather, the problem is the conditions under which so many of us are forced to live. We identified a society in which welfare is a far cry from improving the well-being of people, old and young alike.

Although we were not a large group, it was evident that our educational work in schools, community colleges, classes in the social science departments of universities, and church and community groups was helping to alert many others to the realities of growing old in a society where material gain seemed to be the most important social priority.

Invariably, the need for contact and communication across the generations would come into the discussions that were always a part of our presentations. Sometimes people made suggestions about how this could happen, or how it was already being done. We heard of phone friends or of Sunday afternoon gatherings of old and young people alone in big cities or small centres.

One time, when we took our materials around to schools to talk about the problems of the very old with the very young, a group of teachers asked us to put together an educational kit on growing old. They wanted some basic information and facts so that they could teach more about aging. We decided to make the production of this kit our next project, and used it to present some of our growing concerns: about the negative images of old age in our society, the segregation of old people, and the mistaken equation of sickness with old age. Once the kits of printed information, photographs, and ideas for education on aging were produced, they too met with an enthusiastic response.

Establishing a Climate for Change

Over these years I was involved with both the DEC collective and the work of DEA. As I moved into my seventies I found that though the work was often tiring I could still manage it, and the important thing was that I was not alone: There were other DEA members in the same age bracket. One of them, Duff, was the narrator of our slide-tape shows. At one point we had thought of looking for a professional script reader but I am glad we didn't, because many people have remarked on the excellence of her work. Another was Dr. Gordon Struthers, then over eighty, who had spent much of his life in China. He was invaluable in helping with materials, information, and pictures for *These Old Ones*.

Clearly, old people, if physically able and so inclined, can be and are involved in church or community undertakings, like delivering meals, driving people to hospital, or helping with an agency phone. Those in DEA who were less able to move around outside their home environment took on phoning, mailing, or assembling materials for a newsletter, jobs that could be done at home or on a once-a-month basis. Certainly, DEA members had a wide range of abilities and interests. What we all had in common was the fierce desire to use these abilities to make changes we knew were needed in the quality of life for all of us, old and young. DEA seemed like a means of helping ourselves to take the steps that could make our wishes come true. It was in itself a move by older people to consciously break down the barriers between generations and to debunk the myths about aging.

When we met we talked about the negative images of old age being presented in everyday society; how mandatory retirement often forces us to feel devalued, useless, unneeded in the scheme of things; the unfairness of the economic situation experienced by many people, especially women, in their later years; the attitudes in society that seemed to be robbing old people of their independence. We talked about how we were losing our sense of playing a meaningful role in the ongoing affairs of life, how we were losing the positive self-image that goes along with a feeling of contribution to society. We realized that within a system that classifies and categorizes, individual people become digits known by number. There is a disturbing lack of choice in all areas of life, and many old people find that their eagerness for independence is continually eroded. Some are greatly tempted to finally agree that old age – and we ourselves – are a problem.

Acceptance of the status quo takes many forms for old people. One is the urge to say, "Let's sit back and enjoy life. We've earned this and more." Another is the fatalistic "What can I expect? I'm old." Such attitudes lead to a dangerous acceptance: that old people just need to have things done for them, that we will not or cannot do things for ourselves or others. There is a tendency never to question the established ways of doing things.

"People of the present nursing home generation are so compliant," says Trish Spindel, who joined Concerned Friends of Ontario Citizens in Care Facilities when her grandmother was summarily ejected from a nursing home because she required more care than the home was willing to give.[2] Those of us who undertook the work of DEA did not think we should accept things as they are laid out for old people. We decided that social policy must consider the well-being of all people, must consider our unused possibilities and responsibilities. We must all be freed from the divisions that separate us, divisions of age, income, racial background, and gender.

In Canada it seems that we don't know what to do with old people but we don't want to do without them. Our numbers are useful at election time – we get offered a ride to the polling booth, and sometimes polls are set up right in a senior citizens' building. Unfortunately, that's often the last we see of our benefactor until another election rolls around. Although there is talk of the "problem of the elderly", we don't seem to realize what the real problem is. At DEA, we concluded that the whole mindset of our present society is flawed.

Old age is a legitimate part of life, with its own tasks as well as its own needs. The needs are for adequate income, affordable housing, proper education on preventive health measures, or facilities like day hospitals and day care in multi-service centres. More than anything else we need the recognition of old age as "a part of", not "apart from", the society we live in. We need a recognition by society and by ourselves that being old is just as much a part of the life process as being young. Such recognition could help us who are old to be more aware of our responsibility to carry out tasks that our very "living more years" may have fitted us to do. There needs to be thinking about and sharing of the wisdom we have gleaned. That might lead us to embark on new careers; to learn new skills; to gain new insights into our own lives and the lives of those around us. This new insight could help us to understand how to bear and share with others the loss of old friends and the making of new ones, how to prepare ourselves and our families and friends for the inevitable death. Society must be made aware of these needs and tasks, and pushed to take up its responsibility for establishing a climate in which they are met. We, the old ones, with all our experience and knowledge, must be the prime movers in this.

Leaving DEA

Since 1973, soon after joining the DEC collective, and before DEA was an idea, much less a reality, I've been aware of some hearing loss. In 1974 I availed myself of a good hearing aid and it helped some, but my young friends in DEC had to make special efforts to speak so that I could hear. In spite of their understanding and mighty effort to help me, my frustration with not hearing was always close to the surface.

Although I wear my hearing aid all the time and keep it in good repair, it seems I am incapable of picking up a certain pitch of sound, which unfortunately includes a good many of the voices I want to hear. I am told that hearing aid manufacturers are working with electronics experts to develop electronically-assisted hearing aids to allow such sounds to be picked up. It would be great, if this worked, to once again be part of all that's going on around me.

Because of this hearing problem, however, I realized that meetings were becoming impossible, and I finally had to give up my cherished place in the DEC collective. I still have contact with some of the people there, although the organization has grown tremendously. Together with those who have left DEC, they continue to be a valuable reference group for me.

I continued to work with DEA, but I was away from its activities and meetings for rather long periods while visiting my daughters in Africa. These absences tended to isolate me from DEA members and the group's activity. This, combined with a bout of illness and my hearing loss, changed my relationship with that group, too, and it became clear to me that I had to end my association with DEA. In spite of the heavy investment I had made in time, thought, and energy, and although much had been accomplished in our work of education for aging, my hearing loss, poor physical health, and unrealized goals were crowding me towards a point where my usual well-being would be in jeopardy.

It was time for me to make another change, and this was no less difficult than earlier changes in my life. Perhaps because it was so hard, my decision was over-long in getting made. Even when I finally made it, although I was physically away from the work I'd been doing, I found it difficult to live with the "finis" I had written to those ten years. Later, a friend pointed out that I was grieving – a normal reaction after the loss of something very dear – even though the loss had been the result of my own decision. She was probably right, but it took me a long time to understand that, and meanwhile I felt in poor health for quite a few months.

Still, today I have an even greater interest and concern with aging at a time when gerontology has become immensely popular. As I live out my own aging I find that the changes I have made allow me to address this interest and concern in other ways – writing being one of them.

Doing a workshop on aging with elementary school students in Toronto in the late seventies.

7

Aging, Family, and Community: At Home and Abroad

A longer life provides humans with an opportunity to examine their lives in retrospect, to correct some of their mistakes, to get closer to the truth and to achieve a different understanding of the sense and value of their actions.
World Assembly on Aging, Vienna, 1982

OUR DISCUSSIONS following the showings of DEA slide-tape shows often centred on the need for a new sort of family structure, given the distances of many kinds that separate family members. This idea was reinforced by a visit I made to a long-time friend living in a home for the aged in Unionville, Ontario.

I had known Roscoe Chapin since my days at the Indian residential school in Manitoba in the 1930s. Although we had worked together at Norway House, we had not seen each other or been in touch for many years. Now I had heard of him once again and decided, somewhat impulsively, to pay a quick visit.

As I waited for the bus out to visit him, bits and pieces of that earlier time floated around in my memory. I recalled a windy day and his invitation to leave the sewing room for a few minutes to go out on the lake. Roscoe was an expert with a canoe and knew how much I liked to do battle with the waves. Now he was, apparently, well and active at age ninety-five and being honoured by having a scholarship set up in his name. I wondered how he would be finding life in a home for the aged, one that he had helped to plan years earlier when he retired.

When I got there I couldn't find him, and I realized I should have phoned beforehand to let him know I was coming. When I asked about him somebody told me that he might have gone out for a walk or he might be taking in one of the home's various activities. So, as I looked around for him I had a chance to get a feel for the place. It seemed better than most of the homes I had visited. It was helped out by a beautiful setting – lots of trees – and was an especially good place for walking. There was less regimentation and the residents I saw seemed to be busily following their own pursuits, with assistance if they needed it, and with lots of them apparently making good use of the facilities.

I still couldn't find Roscoe and I began to fear that I would not even see him, let alone have a chance to talk. One last look near the dining room – for the people on his floor had told me he would be there for dinner at five o'clock – and sure enough, there he was coming towards me just as I had seen him many times strolling into the school at Norway House. He had been out for a walk. He said, "I make myself go out for a walk every day," adding with great feeling, "You have to keep going or you rot."

We had only fifteen minutes before he was due at table and I had to leave for the bus, but they were precious moments and we exchanged bits of our experiences. I asked Roscoe whether the home, which had resulted from an idea of his, had turned out as he had hoped. "In many ways yes, but it's different now," he said. "Our families are far away. Our friends are scattered." Perhaps in the early planning he had thought to share life in this home with his wife Etta. But she had become ill with a sickness akin to Alzheimer's, an agonizing situation for them both. She died years before the home was completed.

I mentioned to Roscoe how in DEA's work with students in the schools we often discussed the need for a different kind of family, one that was not necessarily related in the conventional family sense. Such an extended family could allow for interdependence by providing mutual support, and at the same time encourage independence. If and when help was needed it would be there. Roscoe responded with a depth of feeling I cannot express in words: "We need each other."

As I rode back on the bus, I realized that the kind of extended family we'd been discussing was exactly what we had known at Norway House, where distance and weather conditions – "freeze-up" and "break-up", fall and spring – disrupted communications with blood-related family. Being reminded of the warmth and strength of the Norway House "family" had made us more aware of the present need and possible richness of such a relationship. We do need each other ... and could help each other more than we do.

And then I began to think of DEA's work in the schools and the need for communication and contact between the generations. I have experienced something of a new kind of extended family in my work situation, in travelling and living on another continent, and from living in several apartment buildings. Rather wistfully, but with anticipation too, we in DEA often discussed the value of an extended family built on the assumption of old and young people understanding, caring for, and supporting one another for the mutual benefit of all.

We wondered if the extended family of yesteryear was really the unmixed blessing we sometimes think it was; or the recent nuclear family such an unmitigated disaster. Now it seems clear to me that what we need to know and do is related to what we think a community is and how it helps or hinders the people in it. I don't exactly know how such knowledge and action can come about. But it seems plausible that we who are old might remember the kind of close neighbourliness we knew in a rural environment and try to help a similar type of friendliness grow

in our apartment buildings, in our clubs, and in our relationships with younger people – even though we live in a world that
too often alienates and intimidates us all. Some in DEA and others in the wider community were experiencing and contributing to this kind of helping of one another.

In my own work, in my living arrangements, and in contacts
in other parts of the world, I've been fortunate enough to discover "family" in unexpected places. I live within a small community of friends, many of whom are less than half my age.
When I get sick or need a hand moving something, there is
usually someone I can call on to help out. Their "work" helping out has no wage value and most of them have other jobs.

Unlike many old people, I am not (yet) socially marooned
within my own age-set, generation, cohort – call it what you
will. I don't feel I'm just being visited out of a sense of obligation when friends drop by. At the same time, I get out a lot. I
guess what I'm trying to say is that I participate in the everyday
life of the society around me, and I do it on several different levels. This is something old people have to do.

Ideally, this participation should offer the possibility of a
wage. I am fortunate because I have a small pension income to
supplement my old age security benefits. This is in large part
due to my return to paid work after the Canada Pension Plan
was in place. As well, my husband was a minister and I a lay
worker in the United Church of Canada, which had its own
very sound pension plan, integrated with the CPP. It is sad but
true that my situation is better than that of many older women
because of my background and the simple facts of being Anglo-
Saxon, educated, and white. When I see the old women –
women my age – staring blankly at the television in an old age
home or shuffling along the street checking out the garbage, I
sometimes think, "There but for fortune...."

Although some older people dislike apartment living, I have
found many aspects of it that I like and people who are often
helpful. Each of the three buildings I have lived in seemed at
first to be barren and unfriendly, but this has not lasted. You
have to make an effort to reach out, for, as Roscoe had said,
"We need each other."

I remember an incident when I returned from six months in

Africa. It had been a gruelling flight and the arrangements for someone to meet me at the airport had not worked out. I got to the door of my building, put down my luggage, and started to search for my keys when a pleasant voice behind me said, "I've got my key. I'll do it."

Do it he did, picking up my luggage, ringing for the elevator, and holding the door until I had got on. When I got to my floor he picked up my luggage and carried it to my apartment, waited until I had the lights on, and said goodnight. What a blessing for me! His kindly help was just what I needed to keep me on track after eighteen hours of airports, planes, lineups, and the disappointment of having no one to meet me. Although I did not remember seeing him before, now he and his apartment mate are good friends of mine and of many others as we have lived through various battles trying to keep the rent down, helping neighbours, and discovering common interests. For me the people in each of the buildings I have lived in have been friends, and in a way like family.

What Is ... What Could Be

DEA's educational resource *In Our Own Homes* attempts to acquaint viewers with some of the alternatives that we discovered through our work.

In some cities the by-laws allow – or a group can get them changed to allow – the rental of a large home where a number of people can live together, sharing the rent, work, and household expenses, where they can be subsidized by government. This kind of venture turns out to be a much less costly process than building a home for the aged.

Co-operative housing programs are available and varied. One I went to see involved a group of retired or about-to-be retired business people who had made plans to build an apartment complex with affordable rentals. They knew what their income would be, planned accordingly, and were able to overcome the governmental roadblocks to such an undertaking.

The presence of a multi-service centre in a community makes it possible for more people to remain in their own homes or to continue living with family members, except in cases where very heavy nursing care is required. It is much less costly and more accessible to have a variety of activities and services available in a central place than it is to provide these things individually.

Day-care centres for old people, within a home for the aged if you like, or in a public building already used and centrally located, make it possible for a family member to continue to care for a loved one. Even for old people whose physical condition requires a certain amount of therapy, a day hospital in a community works wonders. I saw a good example of this on a working trip to Winnipeg in 1984.

I stayed with my sister-in-law Daisy, who was over eighty and living in her own home. The man next door was 104 years old and involved in a day-hospital program. He sometimes worked in Daisy's garden and also tended his own allotment garden, sharing produce with the neighbours. Three days a week the day-hospital program bus picked him up, took him to the hospital, and brought him home again. The program provided a health check and various forms of therapy. I saw a teddy bear he had made and given to Daisy for Christmas, a very fine piece of work.

His wife, much younger, was able to help – if he allowed it. He seemed to me to be very domineering, someone who insisted on being the boss, which didn't always turn out for the best. Although he could get by on his own, he liked his wife to be around to provide help if and when needed. This could be difficult, day in and day out, so the trips to the hospital program gave them both space for their own pursuits. The information I gleaned from observation and conversation with Daisy was that the day hospital program was not only important to the old man but also to his wife, who needed a break from his constant demands. The gardening was a blessing for such a restless, energetic person. It was a community program that worked.

Another one of my explorations came out of an invitation to join the folk from Creative Retirement Manitoba in taping a program being presented by a small group of retired people. They were entertaining another group of old people at a luncheon. Of the sixty people there, entertainers and audience, no two were a bit alike in appearance, actions, reactions, health, mobility, or appreciation of what was going on. What they had in common was being over fifty-five. The entertainers used choral reading as a medium for their contribution, and the entertained seemed to enjoy it. One woman said to me, "We work very hard all year to raise money to help where it is needed. This luncheon and its fun is our one break!"

If we are going to get into the struggle to find better ways for old people in our society, there are positive models that we can look to. On a visit to my home town of Killarney, Manitoba, in the late 1970s, I looked at a rent-geared-to-income project for old people, called Willow Lodge. It consisted of row housing, on ground level, with the fewest possible steps. It enabled people to live separately and still have close contact with families. They could shop, pick up their mail, continue with painting and other crafts, as well as remain involved in voluntary work in the community. The residents had access to a common kitchen and dining room for large gatherings. Outside there were garden plots.

The residents each had a self-contained suite and could bring along some of their own furniture. When I was there, a non-resident caretaker came in each day to help with heavy tasks. A resident manager looked after admissions and change of residency, arrangements for family parties, and other details. Residents themselves did the "in-house planning" in conjunction with the manager. As a result of all this, for people living in Willow Lodge there seemed much less of the daily trauma that so often characterizes an old person's move to a totally strange new institutional setting.

When I went back to Willow Lodge some eight years after my first visit, I was still just as impressed. In fact, I was able to visit with the same person I had talked to on my previous visit. Now, at eighty-six, she was still well and able to be on her own. She had her own organ in her room, and often played both for personal enjoyment and for others who liked to hear the music.

What most struck me about Willow Lodge was that the residents could keep on doing, to the extent of their capabilities, what they had always done. They were not separated off from family and community in a way that would stigmatize them. There was a climate of supportive understanding of when to help and when to just simply be there. The project recognized that many old people want to continue to contribute to the society around them, and that they may need some help to do so as the limitations of the later years overtake them.

Killarney already had a relatively long-established Home for the Aged. Its newer hospital came equipped with a chronic care wing that replaced the small private nursing home where Father lived the last days of his life. The day I arrived, in the early 1980s, a large new public apartment building also opened. A non-profit endeavour with thirty-four units, the apartment building resulted from the work of a local group called New Horizons (a recreation centre and program for retired people), which had taken a survey of the housing needs of old people in the surrounding area. With help from community organizations, government money was raised and the building erected in record time.

Of course, there are many obstacles standing in the way of such projects. Finding and being able to purchase the land in a suitable area is difficult, since being close to the daily life of a community requires being right in its heart, where real estate is likely to carry a high price and be coveted by the developers of condominiums and the like. In the case of non-government groups like churches and service clubs there is often a lack of knowledge about how to work with the several levels of government involved. Such expertise is essential in establishing housing for old people or affordable housing for any age group, in fact. Too often a group that wants to provide suitable and affordable housing seeks advice from the wrong sources. They ask help from experts who are more concerned with their status as developers of beautiful properties than with the needs of old people.

Perhaps what we have to do is borrow from the experience of a group of young quadriplegics who were facing life in chronic care institutions. Through rehabilitation programs this group had purposefully received detailed training to live as independently as possible. But their efforts to find suitable housing led nowhere. The waiting lists were so long that it seemed many of them would likely become old and die of natural causes before something became available.

As this group of severely handicapped people – who share the same disadvantages as many people over eighty – began to look for alternatives to continued life in chronic care facilities, they were told by the government that help was not available for individuals. It was suggested that if a group of twelve or more could work together they might be able to secure some funds. "They wanted us to do all the work," one said cheerfully. "And we did. And, at the same time we were learning the facts of life."[1]

If people with such physical handicaps could win the fight for suitable housing, surely we old people can make more effort to obtain the help required and make sure there is a reasonable supply of housing for all of us who cannot bear the thought of life in an institution. Too many of us have accepted the facts of life as unchangeable. We don't explore available alternatives or insist that some alternatives *be made* available. Too often we attempt the individual approach. A strongly integrated group, even if it is small, can get a lot done, when a single voice is not heard.

Perhaps in the future old people will not go along with the preconceived notions of what they need and want. They will insist on getting what they themselves *know* they need and want, whether it is for themselves or for others less able to take up the struggle for human dignity and well-being. I hope. I hope. I hope.

Aging: The International Issue

With both my daughter Judith and my friends at DEC working on international issues, and with the trips I've made abroad, I suppose it is not surprising that I began to compare issues of aging in Canada with situations in Third World countries.

In fact, I knew from my earlier work and had continued to find that aging has been and is extensively discussed and analysed on an international level. In 1971 Canada and Malta co-sponsored a United Nations resolution requesting the UN Secretary-General to undertake a thorough "study of the changing socio-economic and cultural roles and status of the aged" and to develop "guidelines for national and international action related to the needs and role of the elderly and aged in society".[2]

The study was completed two years later and submitted to the General Assembly, where the Canadian delegate commented on its excellence. The report pointed out what observers of the changing position of old people had already realized. The world's population was becoming older. Societies everywhere were undergoing profound demographic changes. More people were living longer. There was a general greying of the population.

The delegates assembled in New York were also told that these changes would pose serious challenges. And there were said to be serious contradictions. Technological advances in developed countries were tending to displace older people in the production lines, and at the same time society was more and more able to support "its non-productive members" through its capacity for increased production. The technological advances had also made possible improvements in the "standard of living, mobility, communications and other facets of life for the aged as for other groups". But older adults weren't able to take advantage of the advances because of "economic deprivation". In addition they were being isolated and socially distanced from younger generations because of the effects of urbanization. The report concluded that similar problems were occurring in developing countries:

> Lengthening life expectancy, coupled with degenerating social and economic aspects associated with aging, could result in a steady worsening of conditions for the aged in the developing countries as has been the case in the developed countries.[3]

Appropriate action to prevent such deterioration must be taken, the report stated. Appropriate action, however, has not been immediately forthcoming from international institutions.

For example, in the 1982 World Assembly on Aging held in Vienna two background studies on the development and humanitarian issues of aging overlooked the context out of which these issues emerged – the society we live in and its underlying assumptions about old age. These were not examined and the real challenge – transforming a society in which material things take precedence over people – was not taken up.

The studies placed the lives of old people in both the developed and underdeveloped worlds in either of two compartments. They centred humanitarian issues around how to improve the delivery of services to the dependent elderly. They described development issues based on the way the dependent elderly were going to affect the economic picture adversely as their numbers rapidly increased.

The pre-Assembly news I saw was not encouraging. I noticed an article about the meetings in the local paper. The headline was "Problems of the Elderly to Grow Worldwide". Once again, the problems of the elderly were underlined. It was a familiar litany.

Canada is not alone in facing a population explosion among the elderly.... The coming crisis, simply put, is that the baby boom generation is growing older as subsequent smaller generations approach adulthood, so that the future Canada faces, along with most of the world, is one in which increasing numbers of elderly will depend upon a proportionately shrinking workforce.... For the first time, demographic projections concentrating on aging have been made beyond the year 2000, yielding figures that are at best disheartening and at worst frightening.[4]

It appeared to me that the changes being discussed in Vienna were seen in negative terms. Did the changes have to be so disheartening and frightening?

The situation of old people in Canada is hardly unique to this country. In the same way that individual people become older, entire populations age as the average age increases. While not as "old" as many countries, Canada is now regarded as having an old population because over 8 per cent of its people

are past the magical age of sixty-five. But we cannot really separate individual aging from population aging since the results of
each phenomenon are inextricably woven together.

From Ghana to China to Swaziland

In 1968 I found myself on another continent for the first time in
my life. As a complete change from what I was doing in the
national church office, I accepted my daughter Judith's invitation to visit her in Ghana where she was involved in a program
to help rural people displaced from their homes by the construction of the Volta River hydro-electric dam project at Ako-
sombo.

It was a unique experience – my first time on the African
continent and a non-tourist chance to see how ordinary people
lived. So I tried to get some insights into what it was like to
grow old in Ghana. Whenever I asked, the inevitable reply was
that old people lived with their families. There was no
problem.

What I saw gave me a different answer to my question. I did
see old people with their families in both the cities and the
countryside. If there was enough money and the old people
were in good health there didn't appear to be too many problems. There were usually enough tasks to be done that old
people still had some meaning in their lives. But if an old person were ill or disabled, life became fairly empty. Where lack of
money was also a factor, their plight was pitiful – begging was
the only way to stay alive.

In Ghana I learned about sewing meetings. An invitation for
one was pinned to the screen door of Judith's house, inviting us
to come because "some mystics were to be performed". What
were those mystics? Judith didn't know, nor I. We went, and
the sewing was going on – small garments for children, items
for the house, market bags, and the odd gift. Of course, I didn't
understand the words being spoken but it seemed similar to the
kind of news exchange at a sewing meeting anywhere, no mystics so far. Then the sewing was put away, the room was re-

arranged, and I was led to a central place in the circle. I wondered, what now?

Through Judith and Grace, a young Christian community worker, a general welcome was extended to me. Then each of those present, in turn, presented a small gift – tomatoes from her garden, a few eggs – in token of the esteem in which Judith was held and thanks for her being there ... a handshake and a smile. Then it was my turn to respond. I couldn't swallow the lump in my throat, at first, and the tears overflowed. I managed to catch Grace's hand and stumble my thanks and appreciation for their welcome and their care for Judith in the work they were doing together.

A few days before, I'd seen these women dancing at a celebration and noted one in particular. Judith explained that she was the queen mother, who among other things had responsibility for choosing the chief. After the sewing meeting it seemed the women would sing and dance the same song when we went outside. The sponsors in America, a church there, wanted a picture. Making sure their colourful head-dress was in place and the handkerchief so much part of the dance was ready, they went out one by one shaking my hand again ... all but the last one ... the queen mother. She came to me and lightly, but with such tenderness, touched my face with her delicately-scented handkerchief as if to dry my tears. And I knew again that messages from the depth of one to another don't always need words.

In 1974 I had a chance to visit China as part of a group of people from the Canadian Association for Adult Education. I asked to be able to visit and talk with older people there. As one of the older members of the tour group, I experienced the preferential treatment given to old people in the traditional Chinese way. People offered help with stairs. People listened with courtesy and I had the impression that special concern was being expressed for my well-being.

The old people I met and talked with in China seemed to be in good shape, healthy, active, and involved in teaching and passing on skills to others. They were also very much involved in caring for each other. Because the physical necessities were supplied by the government, old people were free from fear of destitution and proudly made whatever contribution they could to the general good of all. This help seemed to be expected by the younger people, who were proud of the accomplishments of the older members of the family. Old people in the areas of China we visited had access to health clinics and preventive health education and they participated actively in daily exercise programs.

In China, one day I saw a group of old people in Wusih resting on the steps of the plum garden. I wanted to take a picture of them but how could I ask permission when I couldn't speak one word of Chinese? They seemed to understand my gestures towards them and back to my camera. Smiling, one of the group quickly arranged himself and the others and then nodded to me to go ahead. Needless to say I treasure that snap, even if I'm the world's worst taker of pictures.[5]

Some years later, in 1979, I found myself back in Africa, again visiting family. This time I was on the other side of the African continent and further south, in Swaziland, where my youngest daughter, Mary, was living and working with her husband in the office of an asbestos mine. I again had the chance to visit both towns and rural areas and talked to old and young people, including taking in some meetings Mary and her husband set up for me at the university.

In these places I saw that old people continued to be part of the family structure, and there appeared to be almost total unawareness that there might soon be a problem for them. But to an outsider it was obvious that the way of life in the countryside was changing fast and that this would have serious consequences for old people and their family situations. Swaziland is a very small country and more and more land is being taken up by industrial developments. People are being forced into cities where there is no provision for housing, income security, food, and clothing. With young family members employed in one industry or another at low wages, old people were starting to become isolated. Many would obviously soon become destitute.

When I was back in Swaziland in 1980-81, on a second visit, I saw and heard that still more land was being taken over by companies and that industrialization had continued. More people were moving into the cities and large towns. In the small village where I was staying I had a delightful, thought-provoking experience. One sizzling hot day I walked down to the shopping area with the promise of a lift back when I was through with my errands. While waiting for the car to arrive I sat down on some rough wooden steps and took in the passing scene. A Swazi woman who seemed older than I walked by several times. I smiled and she smiled back. Then she touched her head and pointed up to the sun, which seemed to make everything throb in its glare. She crossed the road and sat in the shade. A few minutes later she came across to me again, pointing to the sun and my head and to the shade across the street. I got the message. At the risk of not seeing the car I was waiting for, I crossed with her into the cool of the shade. There we sat, unable to talk to each other but still sending and receiving messages of good will – just as in visits I had made to Ghana and China years before.

Perhaps it is the accumulated folk knowledge and understanding from our years of living that makes such communication possible, even without words. Whatever the reason, through these unique experiences I became very much aware of a common bond among country women the world over, even when language was difficult and communication took place without spoken words. That bond comes to us now as a precious gift from women like our grandmother McKnight, mother Edith, and some of her Women's Institute friends – no longer among us, in a physical sense; and as my experiences revealed quite clearly, that gift has been received and is very much a part of women all over the world. It is timeless and ageless and holds in place simple, but exceedingly important and valuable, expressions of belief in human beings.

Among the Old in Mozambique

After my 1979 visit to Swaziland I went on to nearby Mozambique to visit my daughter Judith, who worked in the Ministry of Education and Culture. I had sent information through TCLSAC* to the Director of Social Action in the Mozambican government about my work in Canada in the field of aging. I wanted to be able to speak about this work with people doing similar work in Mozambique. I had also sent along a copy of the DEA slide-tape show, *These Old Ones*.

When I arrived in Mozambique I was told that whenever I was ready arrangements could be made to respond to my request to learn more about work with old people in that part of the world. After getting to know my way about I set up a meeting to work out some sort of schedule. I'll never forget the meeting. From my conversation with the Director of Social Action I learned that I would be free to visit old people in several provinces.

I was impressed by how well-organized things were in spite of shortages of nearly every resource. These positive impressions grew even stronger when the director told me that old people in Mozambique were seen as a social resource in a way perhaps unique in Africa. The social disintegration resulting from the growth of cities, migration to neighbouring South Africa, and ten years of colonial war had tended to break down the extended family and diminish its capacity to care for older people. Thousands of old people had been abandoned and could no longer care for themselves on their own. The government, although virtually without material resources, was attempting to make sure that these people did not end up as they do in so many other societies, begging and living in the streets. In Mozambique in 1979 there was still begging, but the government was working as quickly as it could to eliminate it, I was told.

Much of this effort consists of creating, for old people, self-sufficient institutions based on artisan activities, agricultural

---

* TCLPAC had become TCLSAC (Toronto Committee for the Liberation of Southern Africa) after the Portuguese colonies had gained their independence in the mid-1970s.

production, and links with child-care centres. In building links between old and young, the aim is to enable old people to transmit their skills to the young generation and at the same time allow old people to be constantly exposed to the stimulus that comes from being with children. The success of these efforts has been mixed; there are some projects housed in former institutions with their familiar orientation towards dependency and charity. In these, it is more difficult to make the needed changes towards a new concept of life for old people.

On one of Judith's holiday trips I was able to visit two residential institutions in the capital city of Maputo, as well as an old people's village near Massinga in Inhambane province and a newly built residential facility just outside of Xai-Xai in the province of Gaza. The main impression I came away with centred on the simplicity of the buildings, which provided well for the functional aspects needed for everyday living. I couldn't help making a negative comparison with our often over-elaborate buildings in Canada, where I'd heard residents complain that "life in these places is lonely and uninteresting".

I heard no such comments in Mozambique, and the liveliness and energy of the people were quite evident. You could not fail to see how glad the people were to have shelter and to sense their pride in contributing to the well-being of their residential community by growing fruits and vegetables, raising livestock, maintaining the buildings, and helping to prepare and serve the meals. Everyone seemed to contribute to the limit of their ability.

Each time I arrived at one of the places where old people were living I was soon caught up in this climate of mutual support. The old people welcomed me enthusiastically and were keen to show off their proud achievements. Of course, language was a problem. In the Old People's Village near Massinga, the old people did not speak or understand Portuguese, the language of the former colonial power and the lingua franca in Mozambique. The young woman who was in charge there spoke virtually no English. To communicate I had to talk to my daughter Judith, who translated into Portuguese for the young liaison woman in charge, who in turn translated into the dialect of the people.

This rather laborious process seemed to work out well as we carried on the formal welcome and greeting part of our visit. When we were invited to join in the singing and dancing that are so much a part of African culture, the language problem disappeared and communication was very simply alive in this small celebration of their freedom and the first visit of Canadians to their village.

Meetings and gatherings in Africa are often held in the cool shade of the spreading branches of a large tree. As we drove up to this old people's village we could see people making their way to the huge baobab tree from various directions. A large group carrying their tools over their shoulders came from the garden plot where they had been working. Others trickled in from the cooking area and a citrus grove. I saw one woman, immaculate in a light blue pantsuit, sliding on her behind across the ground from her house to the shade of the tree. A young man was led to the tree by an old man, each one holding onto one end of a long stick, the Mozambican version of the Canadian white cane.

Later, during the dancing, I saw the young man stand up as if he would like to join in. The woman in the blue suit slid over and smoothed out the ground in front of him, lifted his shoes out of the way, gave him a little nudge and he began to dance, first by himself and then with others who seemed to have received a silent signal to join him. No need for him to see the dance, I realized, and no need for the woman to be able to walk to help him get started.

During that 1979 visit I talked with the government people in charge of social policy in the new Mozambique, in particular about their policy for old people. I was able to visit a variety of settings where the policy was being implemented. Basic in the policy was the premise that public assistance is necessary but, of itself, not enough. As well, the attitude and organization of society must be such as to make it possible for all members of that society to contribute in every way they can, whatever their age or state of health. When assistance is needed it is not seen as charity doled out to a non-productive individual, but rather is the outgrowth of a pattern of co-operation and caring.

Now it is with heavy heart that I remember those exciting

moments of conversation with government officials and the depth and warmth of my experiences with those strong and gentle people ... the old ones of Mozambique. What of them now – in face of the reality of the on-going war of destabilization, of drought and famine? Almost certainly many have not survived. But the struggle toward the goal of co-operation and caring will not be given up. Independence in one's own country is too precious to be lost again, no matter how long and hard the struggle.

The Colonization of the Old

Before I left Canada for Mozambique in 1979, Judith knew I wanted to do some writing. When I arrived in Africa I found she'd put a desk in my room and that she'd also managed to come by a desk lamp – each item in short supply there. One day, sitting at that desk, a look around my room started a train of thought. Judith had pinned a collage of our family snapshots on the corkboard at one side of the desk, and over on the other side there was an old photo of a family picnic at Killarney Lake in 1912. Directly in front of me was a poster depicting the anti-colonial struggle of the Mozambican people. It said:

> We grow up, it's true Some before, some afterwards, Each with his own past But now The Revolution rules our senses We are a million voices, a millions hands united and what matters is not what you or I want But what WE want and this is how the road is....

So much history – of people, communities, and nations – was there before my eyes, reflected in that poster and those photographs. As I thought about my lifetime as part of this history, I recalled brief glimpses I'd had of a kind of world where "what WE want" would take precedence over what you or I want, where trust and confidence in each other would govern our actions and lead us into a new way of loving and living together.

The situations from which these glimpses had come were real, but tentative, steps to initiate and gain support for a way of living that often flew in the face of established policy, whether it was a new curriculum in a church education program or a housing or recreation program in the community for people young or old. Here, in Mozambique, after a long history of building campaigns against colonialism, enough of the people had joined the movement for freedom that independence was won in 1975. The pride and excitement of that accomplishment was very evident in 1979 and – as had happened after my 1974 visit to China – the experience led me to some deep and disturbing thoughts about our own situation in Canada. In particular, I wondered about the fate and the energies of old people, the fastest-growing segment of the population in Canada. Surely this group had the potential to influence policy in regard to the everyday issues that all of us, old or young, must face.

In my work I had seen very little evidence that our potential power was being realized or used to address the policies around adequate income, housing, choice of retirement time, accessible services ... the list goes on. I had seen several kinds of division: *age divisions*, young and old in different life-styles, not knowing that their separation wasn't good for either group; *gender divisions*, particularly in relation to the money most men have compared to most women; *living divisions*, where men could often maintain their homes for a longer period than women, or if they couldn't, move in with a son or daughter, whereas women seemed more apt to opt for a home for the aged or another institutional setting; *image divisions*, of how old age is seen in men as opposed to how it is seen in women; *status divisions*, where men and women with money, health, professional skills, and the desire can maintain a good measure of control over their own lives, in contrast to the women and men who have none of these assets and who are, whether or not they want to be, in the position of losing control of their lives. In any or all of these divisions, some concern about policy issues could be seen ... but unconcern seemed to be the norm.

It had been my hope that an organization like DEA would be able to stimulate and provoke thinking and discussion around these important issues. I had hoped that we could rally many people, old and young, to speak out for the needed changes and move on towards influencing the policies that so directed how we could live our lives. But I had not heard the "million voices" or seen the "million hands united" proclaimed by the poster on my wall in Mozambique. There was not even a faint resemblance to any such movement towards the changes that are so much needed by so many people.

For the most part what I did see had been evidence that "me and mine" takes precedence here in Canada, without much thought for the consequences. However, through my contact with groups like the Development Education Centre and the Toronto Committee for the Liberation of Southern Africa, and from individuals who commented or raised questions in situations where we were showing the educational resources, I knew that there were people deeply concerned and working hard to help Canadians become more aware of what is going on around us, in Canada and in other parts of the world. For instance, whenever I visit my daughter Brenda and her family in Thunder Bay, Brenda – who works actively in her community and in the church she attends – invariably arranges informal meetings with concerned groups or individuals who want to discuss the ideas we present in our slide-tape shows. Or in another setting – a conference – one or two people will come to me and remark, "I like what you said. Can we talk about it?" For me, these are encouraging signs of awareness and of an interest on the part of some in working towards change in our society.

When I visited Mozambique a second time in late 1980 and early 1981, I was recovering from a severe illness and was not up to trips around the country. In Maputo, where I was staying, I was able to accept an invitation to go to a session at a language institute. The students would in a sense be using me to help improve their English, and the content was to be "growing old". We would look at the slide-tape resource *These Old Ones* as a tool for sparking discussion.

It was a good session. The students worked at translating from English to Portuguese for a woman who was director of the government's program for old people in Mozambique. She had asked if she could come to the class. They translated from Portuguese into English for me when comments or questions came that I couldn't understand. We got into a discussion of aging and in response to their questions about the Canadian situation I tried to get across the idea that old people in Canada were in a way *colonized*.

Although I hadn't really put my thinking into words before, my impressions of the forced institutionalization of old people had been growing. The questions and comments from the Mozambicans and my memory of visits with old people in Mozambique in 1979 strengthened these impressions in my mind. A good deal of what I'd been thinking came out, as I explained that I was not talking about our living in physical institutions, although many old people in Canada do live in them. Rather, there is a different kind of institutionalization at work that involves our minds being taken over so that we accept and do not question what is happening to us. We also do not recognize our responsibility for doing something about it. We have been sucked into a mechanistic way of thinking about life and have developed a kind of colonized mentality.

We see ourselves as powerless, dependent on "them" to do things *for* "us". There are many "thems" in our society. In fact, in relation to aging and old people a new and growing enterprise is in full swing. Most of it is based on the premise of old people as helpless, needing to have all kinds of services delivered to us.

A Call for the Future

The Advisory Committee for the United Nations World Assembly on Aging suggested in 1982:

> The aged should be encouraged and enabled to live and function as normally as possible within their own environment and should be encouraged and assisted to determine their own modes of living. They should also be encouraged and enabled to influence and participate in decisions concerning their own lives and welfare and should, by suitable motivation and meaningful activity, play a creative role in the community. The aged should

be considered a valuable resource and must be assured of social, economic and personal security.[6]

In 1983 a second Canadian Conference on Aging was called to discuss plans for implementing the recommendations of the previous year's World Assembly on Aging. Frances McHale, chairperson of the Ontario Advisory Council on Aging, attended the meetings. She wrote an editorial in the Council's newsletter, sent to everyone in the province over sixty-five. She said:

> The challenge that emerged for all of us attending the Second Canadian Conference on Aging has become an individual and a collective Long Term Goal. Older people in Canada are not a separate group with interests and needs that are different from the rest of Canadian society: they are a vital and valuable part of Canadian society who should be involved in society's decisions.[7]

In 1985, *Convergence*, the International Journal of Adult Education, published a special issue on "Education and Older Adults: Implications of the Age of Aging". Writers from around the world contributed ideas on many aspects of the subject. "Advocacy for the Benefit of All" – a section of the introduction by Margaret Gayfer, the journal's editor – caught my eye.

> What "the age of aging" already shows ... is the visibility of a new generation of older persons who want, and are more able, to assert their needs, identify injustices and inequalities, and press for the acknowledgement and value of their contributions to the nation, the community and the family.[8]
>
> In face of the dangers of segregation of the elderly from the rest of society, we must see the advantages for everyone of the goal of an age-integrated society, if our advocacy is truly for the benefit of all.
>
> Thus the new focus on "education and older adults" is really a common front, a move towards solidarity and mutual support

among generations against discrimination and injustice to insure that all citizens stand to benefit from the equal availability of social and economic security.[9]

It sounds good, but will it happen? Exactly how old people will be empowered to take part in "society's decisions" is far from clear.

Over the past ten years or so I have tried to put my amazement and anger to work to change the mistaken assumptions about aging that are all around us. Through DEA I was involved in a considerable effort aimed at presenting positive images about growing old. I believe that our efforts have not been in vain. We did get financial support for the group. We worked hard at going into schools and talking with students and teachers, challenging negative ideas about aging and negative images of old people, discussing the need for a new type of extended family.

At the same time my hope for the emergence of a national group that would express some of these concerns has not been realized. I have been frustrated by the lack of response from old people themselves, who for the most part seem to accept as perfectly normal what is going on and what is not being done. I am fearful as I look back over the years of my involvement in education for living in the later years. There seems to be so little progress towards the lofty goals so frequently set forward.

Over and over in my head I hear the phrase "reality is a social construct". I am haunted by its significance for our situation. We *have* allocated social values, we *have* spent huge sums of money by allowing our political and governmental institutions to play a critical role that for the most part excludes us older people. Is it all our fault? How did we so easily give up our right to a share in decision-making? We did as we were told. We adapted ourselves to a prescribed system. We didn't question why, as Joseph Tindale and Victor Marshall put it, the "general thrust of gerontological scholarship has been to view any lack of fit between individual and society as requiring changes in the former rather than the latter".[10]

Those of us who are concerned can and must change a

system that puts material possessions and a successful image before quality of life for its people of all ages. But we need another skill as well as the will. We need the ability *to do* what we have willed. We must learn how to plan strategy that will move us from one objective to the next. We must involve all the people we need to help us get where we want to go. We have to learn how to get the money we need. Such skills are part of the available resources but most of us are not using them as much as we could or should if we are serious about improving the quality of our lives.

Some people are doing this. I am constantly encouraged by the knowledge that many intelligent, thoughtful, capable, well-trained men and women are engaged in administrative and educational positions in local communities and churches. They make important contributions for social planning in their particular areas, so that needed changes can be made towards improvement in quality of life for all of us.

Through DEA's work in schools, it became clear that many teachers, too, are putting time and thought into helping their students understand some of the implications of the divisions among us of age, race, gender, and class. They seemed especially glad to find educational resources about old people in Canada, produced and used by old and young people. This is another bit of encouragement to me and to the others who worked on the production of the resources.

It is good to see signs that some people, young and old, are beginning to recognize the need for a different perspective. For example, "Do Seniors Have the Power to Influence the Future?" was the topic of a public forum in the Centre for Creative Living. With a number of other men and women, I travelled quite a long distance to hear the panelists and especially the input from old people in the discussion of this subject. Do seniors have the power to influence the future? It seemed a pertinent question given the prevailing negative images of old people.

A few years ago the *Gray Panther Network* newsletter published the story of one of the group's most active members, Mildred Robbins Sklar. Her list of activities and involvements filled several columns, and her motto was, "Don't work harder. Work smarter." She argued, "What we have got to do is get out to the grassroots people and make them angry at the ways they're being mistreated. People won't do things unless they're angry."[11]

So can older people influence the future? Do we have the power? I think the answer to both these questions is again a decided yes. But too many of us do not make the best use of our power to influence the future. We do not recognize how much what we did or did not do has influenced what is happening today. We have delegated our responsibility to advisory committees or other "thems".

But advisory committees cannot do for us what we should be doing for ourselves. Too often such committees draw their advice from those who are financially secure and fit into the category of successful retirement. As far as it reflects the concerns of the elderly, policy is influenced by the perspectives and concerns of this, the minority of old people. People generally take action to change things in their own interest, so it would be unlikely that affluent seventy-year-olds would support demands for higher succession duties or other taxes on the wealthy in order that all old people could be guaranteed an adequate income.

There also does not seem to be any interest on the part of most old people in what is happening to the income, already inadequate, of single parent families and those families described as the working poor. I'm not sure many of us are even aware of the great number of people both old and young who are without a decent and affordable place to live and without enough money for food.

Of course, there are those among the elderly working hard to discover what can be done to restore old age to its rightful status as a legitimate and even honoured part of the lifespan. For our encouragement, some old people have been, and are, quietly debunking the myths by the way they have lived or are living. One woman active on the Members' Council of the Centre for Creative Living told her fellow members, "I am very pleased with every advancing year. It stems back to when I was sixty. I was upset at reaching that milestone but an older friend consoled me, 'Don't complain about getting older, many, many people don't have that privilege.'"

I can also say that I see and am glad that not all old people have succumbed to the prescribed social image, the prescribed role. Even so, I believe that most of us who do protest our fate do so in isolation. It is my great hope that, while there is still time, more and more of us will refuse to accept what is prescribed for us in our later years. And that more and more of us will, by this refusal, be drawn into a strong and active amalgam of awareness and caring for all the people in our world. We need to put forth a more humane image of what it can mean to be old and alive. We need to be actively shaking things up in the search for a new social definition and a new social reality.

Notes

Chapter 2:
The Realities of Growing Old

1 "The coming old-age crisis," *Maclean's*, Jan. 17, 1983.
2 Barry D. McPherson, *Aging as a Social Process: An Introduction to Individual and Population Aging* (Toronto: Butterworths, 1983), p. 82.
3 See, for example, *The Globe and Mail*, Aug. 28, 1986, p. A4, where it is reported: "People aged 75 and older form the fastest-growing population group in Ontario"; and "A Matter of Care," *Maclean's*, Oct. 6, 1986, p. 50.
4 The Senate of Canada, *Final Report of the Special Committee of the Senate on Aging* (Ottawa, 1966); see also R.E.G. Davis, *Programs on Aging: A Critical Review of the Senate Report on Aging*, Interest Group Papers, Canadian Conference on Social Welfare (Ottawa: The Canadian Welfare Council, 1966), p. 3.
5 Health and Welfare Canada, *Canadian Government Report on Aging* (Ottawa: Minister of Supply and Services, 1982), pp. 43, 92; Health and Welfare Canada, *The Health of Canadians* (Ottawa: Minister of

Supply and Services, 1981), p. 169. Both cited in Dr. Mark Novak, *Successful Aging: The Myths, Realities and Future of Aging in Canada* (Toronto: Penguin Books, 1985), pp. 60-81.

6 Senate of Canada, *Final Report*, p. vi.

7 United Nations, *Selected Documents from the World Assembly on Aging* (Paris: International Center of Social Gerontology, 1984), p. 105.

8 Government of Canada, *Sixty-five and older: A Report by the National Council of Welfare on the Incomes of the Aged* (Ottawa: Minister of Supply and Services, 1984), p. 24.

9 Health and Welfare Canada, *Monthly Statistics: Income Security Program*, Ottawa, January 1987, p. 32.

10 Government of Canada, *Poverty Profile 1985: Estimates by the National Council of Welfare* (Ottawa: Minister of Supply and Services, October 1985), p. 28. See also, Poverty Profile 1986 *(June 1986), p. 6.*

11 Government of Canada, *Sixty-five and older*, p. 26.

12 Statistics Canada, *An Analysis of Expenditure Patterns of the Elderly: Expenditure Patterns of Elderly Women*, Louise A. Heslop, Ottawa, 1985, p. 8.

13 Ontario Advisory Council on Senior Citizens, *Hearing Impairment and the Elderly*, May 1982.

14 Ibid., p. 1.

15 The National Advisory Council on Aging, *Priorities for Action: A Report* (Ottawa, 1981), p. 13.

Chapter 3:
From Growing Up to Growing Old

1 See "Women's Institute show opens," *The Globe and Mail*, Feb. 11, 1982, p. T3.

2 Quoted in Novak, *Successful Aging*, p. 258.

3 Simone de Beauvoir, *Old Age* (London: Penguin, 1977), p. 53.

4 Ibid., pp. 76-77.

5 L. Somers, *Aging in Pre-Industrial Societies*, quoted in J. Myles, "The Aged, the State and the Structure of Inequality in Canada," in J. Harp and J. Hofley (eds.), *Structural Inequality in Canada* (Toronto: Prentice-Hall, 1980).

Chapter 4:
Caring and Retirement: The Rites of Passage

1 McPherson, *Aging as a Social Process*, p. 137.
2 Quoted in William Graebner, *The History of Retirement: The Meaning and Function of an American Institution, 1885-1978* (New Haven: Yale University Press, 1980), p. 232.
3 Quoted in C. Haber, "Mandatory Retirement in Nineteenth Century America: The Conceptual Basis for a New Work Cycle," in *Journal of Social History*, Fall 1978.
4 Quoted in Graebner, *The History of Retirement*, p. 197.
5 Special Senate Committee on Retirement Age Policies, "Retirement: Policies, Pensions and Proposals," pamphlet, highlights of *Retirement Without Tears*, the Report of the Special Senate Committee on Retirement Age Policies (Ottawa, 1979), p. 4.
6 Quoted in "The retirement conundrum," *Maclean's*, March 26, 1979, p. 12.
7 Special Senate Committee on Retirement Age Policies, "Retirement," p. 15.
8 Carol Segrave Humple and Morgan Lyons, *Management and the Older Workforce: Policies and Programs* (New York: American Management Association, 1983), p. 9.
9 Quoted in "The retirement conundrum," *Maclean's*, March 26, 1979, p. 12.

Chapter 5:
The Emotional Maze – Health and the Business of Aging

1 Ad in *Canadian Family Physician*, March 1984.
2 See *The Globe and Mail*, Jan. 30, 1984, p. B4, for both headlines.
3 *The Globe and Mail*, March 9, 1984.
4 *The Globe and Mail*, April 3, 1984.
5 See Senate of Canada, *Final Report*, p. 101.
6 *The Globe and Mail*, Feb. 26, 1987, p. A19.
7 Jean Oda May, "Introduction," in Yasushi Inoue, *Chronicle of My Mother* (New York: Harper and Row, 1982), p. 9.
8 Social Planning Council of Metropolitan Toronto, *Caring for Profit: The Commercialization of Human Services in Ontario* (Toronto: 1984).

9 *The Globe and Mail*, Oct. 31, 1984; see also "Moratorium," *The Globe and Mail*, Dec. 6, 1984.

10 Daniel Baum, *Warehouses for Death* (Toronto: Burns and MacEachern, 1977), pp. 18-19, quoted in Novak, *Successful Aging*, p. 73.

11 Ann Montagnes, "When elderly parents need care," in *Chatelaine*, September 1984, p. 149.

12 *The Globe and Mail*, Aug. 30, 1984.

13 Lewis Mumford, "For Older People – Not Segregation But Integration," in *Community Planning Review*, September 1956, pp. 92, 96.

Chapter 6:
Development Education – and Action

1 *Canadian Welfare Council Bulletin*, May-June 1974.

2 Montagnes, "When elderly parents need care," pp. 49, 156.

Chapter 7:
Aging, Family, and Community: At Home and Abroad

1 *The Globe and Mail*, March 5, 1984, p. M7: "Long Battle: Quadriplegics refuse chronic care, run their own lives."

2 Canadian Association on Gerontology, *Newsletter*, August 1974, p. 4.

3 Quoted in ibid., p. 5.

4 *The Globe and Mail*, July 23, 1982, p. 10.

5 For more on China, see also Doris Marshall, "Living the later years," in *Convergence: International Journal of Adult Education*, Vol. VII, No. 3, 1974, pp. 25-28.

6 Quoted in *UNESCO Adult Education Information Notes*, No. 1, 1982.

7 Ontario Advisory Committee on Aging, *Especially for Seniors*, Winter 1984, p. 4.

8 "Education and Older Adults: Implications of the Age of Aging," in *Convergence*, Vol. VII, No. 3, 1974, p. 3.

9 Ibid., pp. 3-4.

10 Joseph A. Tindale and Victor W. Marshall, "A Generational-Conflict Perspective for Gerontology," in Victor W. Marshall (ed.), *Aging in Canada: Social Perspectives* (Toronto: Fitzhenry and Whiteside, 1980), p. 43.

11 Quoted in *Gray Panther Network*, March / April 1981.

Other Books from

BEN CARNIOL
Case Critical: The Dilemma of Canadian Social Work

ALISON ACKER
Children of the Volcano

CAROLE CONDE & KARL BEVERIDGE
First Contract: Women and the Fight to Unionize

MARTIN SHAPIRO MD
Getting Doctored: Critical Reflections on Becoming a Physician

MICHAEL CZERNY S.J. & JAMIE SWIFT
Getting Started on Social Analysis in Canada

Write for a complete catalogue to:
Between The Lines
229 College Street, Suite 211
Toronto, Ontario, Canada M5T 1R4